Supporting FAMILIES

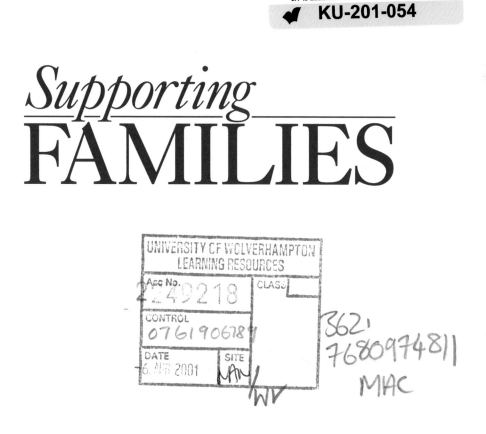
Lessons from the Field

Karen McCurdy / Elizabeth D. Jones

Sage Publications, Inc.
International Educational and Professional Publisher
Thousand Oaks ▪ London ▪ New Delhi

For information:

Sage Publications, Inc.
2455 Teller Road
Thousand Oaks, California 91320
E-mail: order@sagepub.com

Sage Publications Ltd.
6 Bonhill Street
London EC2A 4PU
United Kingdom

Sage Publications India Pvt. Ltd.
M-32 Market
Greater Kailash I
New Delhi 110 048 India

Printed in the United States of America

Library of Congress Cataloging-in-Publication Data

McCurdy, Karen.
  Supporting families: Lessons from the field / by Karen McCurdy,
Elizabeth D. Jones.
      p. cm.
  Includes bibliographical references and index.
    ISBN 0-7619-0678-9 (cl.)— ISBN 0-7619-0679-7 (pbk.)
    1. Child welfare—Pennsylvania—Philadelphia. 2. Child
abuse—Pennsylvania—Philadelphia—Prevention. 3. Family
services—Pennsylvania—Philadelphia. 4. Problem families—Services
for—Pennsylvania—Philadelphia. 5. William Penn Foundation. Child
Abuse Prevention Initiative. I. Jones, Elizabeth. II. Title.
  HV743.P5 M35 2000
  362.76'8'0974811—dc21   00-008120

This book is printed on acid-free paper.

00   01   02   03   04   05   06   7   6   5   4   3   2   1

Acquisition Editor:	Nancy Hale
Editorial Assistant:	Heidi Van Middlesworth
Production Editor:	Elly Korn
Editorial Assistant:	Victoria Cheng
Typesetter:	Marion Warren
Indexer:	Teri Greenberg
Cover Designer:	Candice Harman

Contents

Preface

Since the arrival of the first child, adult caretakers have struggled with the demands presented by their children. In an effort to meet these demands, parents have sought out a variety of supports, drawing on the modeling they experienced with their own parents and extended family members, the availability of support and advice from friends, and assistance provided by local services and related resources. Over the past 30 years, prevention advocates have designed and implemented hundreds of interventions to resolve a parent's lack of knowledge and skills, to create extended networks of formal support, and to alter normative and societal standards for child rearing and education. Whether one talks about the family support movement, the early childhood movement, or child abuse prevention, program planners have struggled with who to include in their target populations and how to structure their interventions.

In 1989, the William Penn Foundation established its Child Abuse Prevention Initiative in the hopes of generating new knowledge on how best to offer meaningful assistance to these families, many of whom lived in Philadelphia's most troubled communities. From the outset, the Foundation's efforts were innovative in two important respects. First, of the initial 14 grantees supported under the initiative, 9 received funding for almost 10 years, providing a unique opportunity to examine the evolution of prevention programs beyond the typical 2- to 3-year funding cycles of most demonstration programs. Second, the Foundation funded an evaluation team at the onset of the initiative to ensure accurate documentation of both the implementation process and service outcomes. As a result of this foresight, the Foundation's efforts offer the field an important reservoir of new knowledge on how best to implement and to assess child abuse prevention efforts in urban communities.

McCurdy and Jones's summary of this history provides many useful lessons for practitioners, funders, policymakers, and researchers. Three of these lessons are particularly useful as child abuse prevention efforts seek to move beyond isolated demonstration efforts and toward a universal system of support for all parents. First, for those who would suggest that families do not want assistance and would find such offers of help intrusive, they would be well served to read the stories told by the families enrolled in the Penn prevention programs. These mothers want for their children the same as most mothers in America—the opportunity for their children to realize their full potential and to live in a healthy and supportive community. At the end of the intervention, many of these parents still struggle, but then, rearing children is an ongoing challenge for every parent. What many program participants have at the end of these interventions, however, is a greater sense that they are not alone and have at least some have faith in their ability to succeed.

Second, the experiences of the William Penn grantees underscore the importance of neighborhood and context in determining prevention's ultimate success. If prevention programs are to maximize their impacts, they must look beyond simply changing the parenting abilities of those they serve. As the Penn prevention program experiences suggest, parents may find it difficult to sustain alternative discipline practices when faced with conflicting messages from family members and neighbors. Recent research in the field of child development, child abuse prevention, and crime prevention has identified specific neighborhood characteristics that strengthen the safety net for children, even when communities share a common level of poverty and internal distress. Specifically, communities in which residents share a common set of values and are willing to provide guidance and supervision of each other's children experience fewer instances of reported child maltreatment and other negative outcomes for children than do communities lacking this level of social cohesion. Successfully strengthening both individuals and communities requires prevention programs such as those funded by the Penn Foundation to establish new partnerships with those institutions and informal social networks that establish a community's collective responsibility toward its children and define a community's sense of collective self-worth.

Last, the experience of McCurdy and Jones in assessing the Penn initiative sends a strong message to researchers regarding the need for diverse analytic methods. The importance of context cannot be overstated in the case of child abuse prevention. Those seeking to develop effective interventions desperately need to know a wide range of information—how families view the service they are being offered, why they accept a given service, why they do not, what other options they see in their communities to support them, and how they view their relationships with their service providers. To the extent that every intervention with a family is unique, evaluation data need to provide guidance as to the specific change mechanisms operating with specific families, under specific conditions.

McCurdy and Jones illustrate how these change mechanisms can be documented through the careful application of differential assessment methods. They have documented progress not only through statistically significant changes on various quantitative measures but also through the stories participants and providers tell in response to structured interviews. Such methods produce data that are more difficult to interpret; some would say data that are more subjective. However, a researcher's theoretical beliefs, professional training, and sense of what is "important" to measure influence all of his or her work, regardless of the research design. The trends and patterns observed and documented in qualitative research are no more or less victims of self-selection and prior beliefs. A finding with a statistic is no more valid or useful for planning than a trend emerging from careful qualitative methods.

Many of those working to strengthen families believe that these efforts need to be taken "to scale" before we can glean the greatest benefits. Such a commitment requires something more than simply implementing isolated well-structured programs. Rather, it requires altering the normative standards new parents have regarding what they can expect by way of support at the time their child is born and as their child grows. It requires understanding how to instill in all parents an interest and expectation for ongoing assistance at the level they need. To accomplish this type of change, prevention programs need to engage and successfully serve not only those who will voluntarily enroll in a demonstration project but also those who are unable to use current support due to a lack of information, a lack of trust, or a lack of sufficient self-worth to demand what is needed to support them as parents. The William Penn Foundation's efforts and McCurdy and Jones's careful and comprehensive analysis provides a useful framework for crafting the interventions and research efforts needed to achieve this comprehensive vision of primary prevention.

Deborah Daro, PhD
Chapin Hall Center for Children
University of Chicago

Acknowledgments

We benefited from the guidance and support of many individuals in this undertaking. First and foremost, the inspiration and enthusiasm of Richard Cox from the William Penn Foundation kept the Initiative funded, ensured that a comprehensive evaluation took place, and focused our efforts on completing this book so that others could learn from this undertaking. We would especially like to thank all the project directors and front-line staff at each of the nine programs for their dedicated service to families and for their willingness to participate in this evaluation.

At the National Committee to Prevent Child Abuse, Deborah Daro and Anne Cohn Donnelly provided conceptual support and invaluable advice on early drafts. Kathleen Casey, Linda Fogarty, Leslie Mitchel Bond, and Saskia Subramanian assisted with data collection, interviews, and analyses. We also acknowledge the assistance of staff from the Institute for Child and Family Policy, Muskie School of Public Service, at the University of Southern Maine. Jean Bessette and Paul Ridlon provided proofreading assistance and Tammy Richards compiled and edited the manuscript. Last, we thank three anonymous reviewers for their insightful comments and suggestions.

CHAPTER 1

Child Abuse Prevention

The William Penn Foundation Initiative

During an interview with the executive director of a well-known child-serving agency, we asked why her agency became involved in child abuse prevention programs. She responded with this example: If we call Child Protective Services and report that a parent is dangling her 6-year-old son out of an eighth story window, they will not respond. But after the mother has dropped the child from the eighth story window, then Child Protective Services will respond.

Although this comment may be disheartening, it is the reality in many cities and towns. As a society, we believe that every child has a right to grow up without suffering from physical, emotional, or sexual harm. The statistics depicting the chaos and destructiveness embedded in family life in the United States are grim. In 1993, 2.8 million cases of child maltreatment were known to local child protection agencies or community sources, including teachers, health care providers, and social service agencies (Sedlak & Broadhurst, 1996). These estimates translate to 1 out of 24 children in the U.S. child population being a victim of child maltreatment. Each day, at least three children die as a result of abuse or neglect at the hands of someone responsible for their care (Sedlak & Broadhurst, 1996; Wang & Daro, 1998). The dominant response to this epidemic has been to intervene with the family only *after* a child has suffered harm. Traditional intervention options range from removing the child from the home and arresting the abuser, to keeping the family together through intensive family preservation efforts. Unfortunately, by the time such families draw the attention of child protective services, the severity and multitude of their problems require an enormous amount of human and fiscal resources to repair the damage.

This book provides an in-depth look at one large-scale, privately funded initiative designed to assist families *before there is a need for child protective services involvement.* Drawing on 6 years of program evaluation data from nine unique prevention programs in the greater Philadelphia area, we present evidence of the short-term and long-term programmatic benefits to parents, especially those with multiple difficulties who are raising their children in deteriorating urban communities. The evaluation findings confirm that voluntary family support services can prevent child maltreatment among high-risk families but that such efforts demand intensive and comprehensive interventions. Although these programs strove to prevent child abuse, each program designed services grounded in a family support approach that emphasized voluntary participation, strengths-based relationships between staff and the families, and community-based outreach. Consequently, the programmatic lessons presented in this book are applicable not only to child abuse prevention programs but to a variety of family support efforts.

THE NEED FOR EFFECTIVE FAMILY SUPPORT PROGRAMMING

The changing nature of child welfare agencies across the country raises serious doubts about the ability of these systems to ensure the safety and well-being of children. Since the inception of the initial Child Maltreatment and Prevention Act, reports of child maltreatment have increased by 300% without a similar increase in funds to respond appropriately (U.S. Department of Health and Human Services [USDHHS], 1998). Recent surveys indicate that resource constraints have forced child welfare agencies to prioritize their definitions of reportable acts of maltreatment and to curtail the types of ongoing services they give to families (USDHHS, 1998). Child welfare agencies are limiting their resources to focus solely on physical and sexual abuse. This narrow definition allows many needy families to fall through the cracks. For example, many child welfare agencies across the country no longer consider neglect to be a confirmable form of child maltreatment. As Kamerman and Kahn (1989) put it, "Doorways for less serious or differently defined problems are closed." Overburdened child welfare systems have limited amounts of resources available for families, so many families only receive a Band-aid solution to their entrenched problems.

In response to the ongoing crisis in child welfare, the 1995 annual report of the U.S. Advisory Board on Child Abuse and Neglect (ABCAN) urged the development of "comprehensive child-centered, family focused, neighborhood based systems of services" to help prevent child abuse and neglect (ABCAN, 1995). Such a system would include informal family and neighborhood support, assistance with difficult parenting issues through community-based programs, and crisis intervention services. Furthermore, the Advisory Board recommended that this system be the foundation of a primary prevention strategy aimed at increasing child safety, improving family functioning, and reducing maltreatment-related fatalities.

Prior to the Advisory Board's recommendations, President Clinton authorized the Family Preservation and Support Act (1993) that provided states with block grants to develop services. Although much of this money went to enhancing family preservation efforts, states also used some of these funds to provide services for families who had not yet become involved with the child protective services system. Family support efforts differed from traditional social service interventions because they were proactive and available to all parents in the community rather than only those families reported for child abuse and neglect. The primary goal was to provide support to families at risk of abusing or neglecting their children. Under the Adoption and Safe Families Act of 1997, Family Preservation and Family Support was reauthorized and expanded for another 3 years.

Welfare reform in the 1990s may increase the need for family support programming. The Temporary Assistance to Needy Families (TANF; Personal Responsibility, 1996) block grant, passed in 1996, replaced the earlier and long-standing Aid to Families with Dependent Children. TANF ended the entitlement to welfare assistance, reduced the amount of funding, and provided new restrictions on its use for states. The two most significant aspects of TANF were the 5-year limit on benefits and the mandatory work requirement after 2 years. In addition, the new legislation gave states discretion over the definition of eligibility requirements and how the funds will be spent. Child advocates are concerned that welfare reform would place even more stress on overburdened families. Likewise, child protection and child welfare agencies would be called on to provide the kinds of family support and prevention services needed for troubled families. In this era of welfare reform, comprehensive child abuse prevention strategies that provide social support, increase child safety, and help families become economically self-sufficient would play an integral role. As states and communities take more responsibility for the safety and well-being of their children, there is an emerging demand for communities to set up a continuum of care for families who may abuse their children. Recognizing the limitations of child welfare agencies to ensure the safety of children, many locales have been moving toward community-based prevention and early intervention family support programs.

Last, there is evidence that child abuse prevention involvement can save money in the long run. Long-term evaluations of home visiting programs have shown that prevention can "pay off" financially, especially if services are targeted to families with the greatest need. Among low-income families, the investment return was $1.80 per family within 2 years after the program ended (Olds, Henderson, Phelps, Kitzman, & Hanks, 1993). Child abuse prevention programs that focus on prenatal care, immunizations, and well-baby checkups have also shown cost savings at $3.00 per every dollar invested (Brown & English, 1994/1998). One comprehensive program for young children living in poverty showed lasting benefits and a significant return on investment. A longitudinal study found a $7.16 return for each dollar invested (Schweinhart, Barnes, & Weikart, 1993). Some of the savings were related to reduced special education and welfare costs and to higher future worker productivity.

Throughout this book, we offer practical guidance for those developing and implementing child maltreatment prevention services for distressed families. As such, we concentrate on the most valuable "lessons learned" regarding how to recruit and engage vulnerable parents into physical child abuse and neglect prevention services, as well as how to enhance the benefits parents can derive from child maltreatment prevention services. This book has five objectives:

1. To illustrate the kinds of short-term and long-term parenting changes high-risk parents can achieve as a result of prevention program participation

2. To discuss the program characteristics most strongly related to improved parenting outcomes among the highest-risk participants

3. To show how the programs were able to recruit and actively engage families with serious parenting issues and limited economic and social resources

4. To share solutions to typical program start-up challenges and continuing implementation barriers

5. To illustrate the internal and external challenges high-risk parents encounter as they attempt to change their parenting practices

THE WILLIAM PENN FOUNDATION'S CHILD ABUSE PREVENTION INITIATIVE

Since its inception in 1945, the William Penn Foundation has championed issues of child health and welfare. The growing problem of child abuse captured the Foundation's attention in 1985. In response, the Foundation initiated extensive discussions about ways to combat the increase in child maltreatment with experts in the field. At that time, public policies toward child abuse focused primarily on identification and treatment of abusive families. Early research suggested that vulnerable families and neighborhoods could be identified and provided assistance before any abuse had occurred (Garbarino & Sherman, 1980). The Foundation soon learned, however, that most families in the Philadelphia area did not have access to prevention services from private, state, or federal sources.

In 1988, the Foundation decided to expand its commitment to improving the lives of children by placing its resources into child abuse prevention programs. With a $6 million grant to 14 child abuse prevention programs located in the Greater Philadelphia area, the William Penn Foundation's Child Abuse Prevention Initiative was launched.

Recognizing the absence of a universally successful prevention model, the Foundation sought programs that would offer a variety of services though focusing on high-risk families. The 14 programs chosen by the Foundation were located in inner-city neighborhoods and declining suburban communities containing disproportionate amounts of confirmed cases of child abuse. These diverse programs provided a range of services designed to improve parenting, including parent education and support groups, home visiting services, counseling, parent-child play groups, and therapeutic child care. After the first 3-year funding cycle ended, the Foundation elected to concentrate its resources on the nine programs providing secondary prevention services in the highest risk areas. The Foundation provided $3.5 million to these programs for an additional 2-year period. The contents of this book focus on the experiences of these nine programs and their participants.

Development of the Initiative

When the Foundation began discussions with child abuse experts in 1985, limited information existed on how to best prevent child abuse. Both psychological and social learning theories of maltreatment had dominated the field, resulting in many prevention approaches focused on the parent. From the psychological perspective, abusive parenting could be prevented if parents gained a better understanding of themselves and their role as parents (Helfer, 1987; Steele, 1976). This perspective led to the use of individual and group counseling services to address any personal and parental functioning issues interfering with effective child rearing. According to social learning theorists, parents tend to raise their children in the same manner in which the parent was raised (Burgess, 1979; Maccoby & Martin, 1983). To reduce or prevent abusive behavior, then, prevention programs needed to educate at-risk parents on more effective and nurturing ways to discipline and care for their children.

Two emerging theories began shaping child abuse prevention efforts around this time period. First, sociologists looked beyond the parent to identify environmental factors contributing to child maltreatment, such as limited financial resources, lack of support from other adults, and restricted employment opportunities (Gelles, 1992). Such evidence helped formulate prevention efforts

designed to provide parents with the economic and emotional supports necessary to parent adequately, including parent support groups and case management services. Last, an integrative approach known as ecological theory moved
the field toward broader conceptions of prevention programs. Theories based on
this perspective posit that the interaction of characteristics of child, parent, family, and community lead to abusive behavior (Belsky, 1980; Bronfenbrenner,
1979). To prevent maltreatment, an array of services or supports needed to be in
place that reduced stressful interactions across these levels. Services such as
parent-child play groups, home visitation, and family schools are often part of
this approach.

Though several theories looked promising, the small number of evaluations
available in 1988 revealed conflicting results (Fink & McCloskey, 1990). No
single prevention approach stood out as the most effective method to improve
parenting. In addition, relatively few programs had shown any success in engaging and serving high-risk populations (Daro, 1988). These findings prompted
the Foundation to announce the availability of funding for innovative child
abuse prevention programs with few specific service requirements. Due to their
interest in providing prevention services to high-risk families, the Foundation
stipulated only three standard criteria for program eligibility in their request for
proposals (RFP). First, the programs had to serve families residing in specific
census tracts. The Foundation selected census tracts that exhibited elevated
numbers of reported child maltreatment cases, high levels of adolescent parents,
and high levels of infant mortality. Second, eligible programs could not serve
families with current involvement in Child Protective Services. This criterion
underscored the Foundation's commitment to prevention and early intervention
services designed to avert a family's involvement with Child Protective Services. Therefore, the prevention services were offered on a voluntary basis; it
was up to the family to decide whether to accept or refuse services. Last, the
Foundation believed that targeting families with young children was critical to
the prevention effort, so they required that programs limit services to families
with a child under the age of 12.

The Prevention Projects

At the time the Foundation implemented the Child Abuse Prevention Initiative, Philadelphia was a city on the decline. With 26% of all households headed
by females, economic distress abounded. In 1986, the Philadelphia poverty rate
of 23.6% was almost twice the 13.6% average for all U.S. cities (Mitchel, 1990).
More than one third of children in Philadelphia lived in poverty as compared to
20% of children nationwide. High rates of teen parenthood and inadequate
health care services had combined to create one of the worst infant mortality

rates in the country. In Philadelphia, 17 out of every 1,000 infants died, though the average U.S. rate was 9.9 per 1,000 (Mitchel, 1990). An astounding 44% of all pregnant women in Philadelphia did not receive prenatal care in 1987 (Mitchel, 1990). Lack of affordable housing along with increasing violence and availability of drugs all helped make Philadelphia a particularly hostile environment for child rearing (Mitchel, 1990).

For families in need of parenting services, help was virtually nonexistent in the Greater Philadelphia area. The child protection agency, the Department of Human Services, funded only one child abuse prevention program for the entire Philadelphia area in the mid-1980s. Some local groups, such as Temple University and the Children's Initiative Project, had begun projects to support at-risk families. For the most part, however, such projects were in the planning stages. Temple University, for example, received a 5-year, federal grant in 1989 to establish a community-based planning and service council to plan, develop, implement, and monitor a model community-based child abuse prevention program in North Philadelphia (Mitchel, 1990). The Children's Initiative Project proposed to coordinate service delivery to families with young children in the West Philadelphia area. Though promising, neither of these two projects offered support services to families in the short term.

Even families verified as abusive under the state's rigorous Child Protective Services laws could fall through the cracks. As reports of child abuse and neglect rose in the 1980s, funding for the identification and treatment of abusive families declined as a result of a cap placed by the state legislature on the principal source of state child welfare funds (Mitchel, 1990). The child protective service system had become crisis driven, with limited resources available for treatment services and even fewer for prevention. Against this backdrop, the William Penn Foundation's Child Abuse Prevention Initiative sought to fill an enormous gap in services for families.

The flexibility of the RFP afforded the potential grantees extensive latitude in structuring services for these families. Consequently, the nine child-serving agencies in Greater Philadelphia funded under the Initiative each featured a distinctive program design. Though the programs all served high-risk families, they provided a range of prevention services to diverse populations. Seven of the programs served inner-city neighborhoods of Philadelphia; the remaining two were located in adjacent suburban communities. Two programs focused on Hispanic communities; two served mainly Caucasian populations, and five offered interventions primarily to African American families. The following section provides a brief description of each program's location, target population, and service structure. A summary of the programs also is presented in Table 1.1. (For detailed descriptions of the programs, see National Committee to Prevent Child Abuse [NCPCA], 1990, 1991, 1992.)

TABLE 1.1 Program Characteristics

Program Name	Location	Core Services	Target Population	Service Length, Frequency	Number of Families Served
Alternative Family Resources	Pottstown: Racially mixed, blue-collar suburb	Counseling, parent-child play groups, support groups, education groups, survivors groups	Low-income and teen parents of children aged 0-11	26 weeks, weekly	42
Asociación de Puertorriqueños en Marcha, Inc.	North Central Philadelphia: Hispanic, low-income community	Home visits (includes assessment, counseling, case management, parent education, and homemaker services)	Hispanic families with children aged 0-11	34 weeks, weekly	61
Congreso de Latinos Unidos, Inc.	North Philadelphia: Latino, low-income area	Parent education, parent-child interaction sessions	Latino families with children aged 0-11	10 weeks, weekly	150
Crime Prevention Association	North Philadelphia: African American, low-income neighborhood	Parent education, support groups, parent-child interaction, counseling, home visits	Low-income families with inadequate health care, children aged 0-11	16 weeks, 3½ times a week	119
Family Services Association of Bucks County	Bristol and Bristol Borough: white, low-income to middle-income suburb	Parent education, counseling, case management, support groups, home visits	Families with school-aged children	22 weeks, bi-weekly	130
Family Services of Philadelphia	Seven inner-city neighborhoods, African American, mixed income	Parent education, support groups	Families with children aged 0-11	10 weeks, weekly	30

Family Support Services, Inc.	Southwest Philadelphia: African American neighborhood	Family School (includes parent education, support, parent-child play group, developmental day care), home visits	Families with "medically compromised" children aged 0-5	30 weeks, weekly	78
Philadelphia Society for Services to Children	Point Breeze, Philadelphia: African American, low-income neighborhood	Home visits, support groups, toy lending library	Pregnant and parenting teens; families with children aged 0-5	26 weeks, bi-weekly	78
Youth Service, Inc.	Mantua, Philadelphia: African American, low-income community	Home visits, parent education, support groups, parent-child play groups, counseling	Families with children aged 0-5	50 weeks, weekly	126

Alternative Family Resources (Alternatives)

Located in Pottstown, a declining working-class community in Montgomery County, Alternatives targeted its prevention services toward low-income families and teen parents. Alternatives offered a comprehensive service package, including home visits in conjunction with the Visiting Nurse Association, parent-child play groups, parent support groups, and groups specifically targeting teen mothers and teen and adult survivors of maltreatment. In addition, participants could receive free transportation services. Alternatives encouraged the families to attend as many services as possible and allowed an open-entry-and-exit service format. The average length of participation for families using services on a weekly basis was about 26 weeks.

*Asociación de Puertorriqueños
en Marcha, Inc. (APM)*

APM offered intensive, home-based services to Puerto Rican families living in an economically depressed community in North Philadelphia. Based on an ecological approach, services were provided by a family preservation team consisting of a social worker, teacher, paraprofessional, and child development specialist. The home visits alternated among these providers and emphasized life skills education, parenting education, parent-child interaction, and homemaker services. APM added a new component at the time of the second round of funding: In response to participant need, APM created a support group for parents of disabled children, led by a therapist. Though APM's model called for 1 year of services, the typical family received weekly services for about 34 weeks.

*Congreso de Latinos
Unidos, Inc. (Congreso)*

Congreso, also located in North Philadelphia, offered structured parenting education classes to families throughout the Philadelphia Latino community. Based on the work of Alfred Adler, the program delivered parent education as its primary method for changing parenting behavior. Congreso offered 10-week education workshops covering a range of parenting topics, with two classes devoted to specific concerns of the participants. After the parenting class ended, parents participated in a parent-child interaction session. During the second round of services, two key changes occurred: Congreso expanded the length of the workshops to 12 to 15 weeks, and Congreso also created a child health service called KidConnection. KidConnection provided health education and resources to parents through workshops. On average, parents at Congreso attended in 10 weekly sessions.

Crime Prevention Association of Philadelphia

Operating in an economically depressed, inner-city neighborhood, Crime Prevention emphasized intensive, group-based interventions. The 12-week "Morning Program" was originally offered four times a week for 4 hours. Each session included a parent education and support component while children received child care, a meal, and parent-child interaction time. An "Evening Program," with a structure similar to the morning program, operated twice a week for 14 weeks. In the second round of funding, Crime Prevention offered the morning groups 5 days a week and added training on life skills to accommodate their new shelter population. Families usually came to the center three or four times a week for about 16 weeks.

Family Services Association of Bucks County (FSA of Bucks County)

Serving two low-income communities in Bucks County, FSA of Bucks County offered three services: (a) a 25-week Family Life Education series covering diverse topics, such as child discipline, finance, and relationship building; (b) home and center-based counseling and case management; and (c) parent support groups. The counseling and case management component had to be reduced from 12 months to 6 months due to large service demands. After the 6-month period, FSA of Bucks County encouraged parents to attend the monthly parent support group. In response to parental demands, the Family Life Education series was modified over the course of the Initiative. In its final form, the course lasted 10 weeks and was offered three times a year. The average parent at FSA of Bucks County received services on a biweekly basis for 22 weeks.

Family Services of Philadelphia (FSP)

Targeting seven inner-city neighborhoods in Philadelphia with elevated levels of reported child abuse, FSP offered parent education workshops called "Family Clubs," in community settings, such as shelters, drug rehabilitation centers, and community centers. The workshops generally lasted for 6 weeks. In addition to education, the workshops included parenting plays used to model positive forms of parent-child interaction. With the second round of funding, FSP expanded beyond mothers as the primary target of workshops to include fathers and grandparents. On completion of the workshops, participants were encouraged to join ongoing support groups or receive counseling on a limited basis or both.

Family Support Services, Inc. (FSS)

FSS provided intensive, center-based services to families of infants and toddlers with health problems in a low-income area of Philadelphia. The "Family School" offered a set daily curriculum, including separate periods for parent education, parent support, therapeutic child care, and parent-child play groups. The Family School operated for 5½ hours, twice a week. FSS also offered limited home visits, primarily as a method to assess the family and enroll them in the Family School. A new innovation for FSS in the second round was the provision of monthly respite child care services for mothers with perfect program attendance. Service sessions generally last from 6 to 12 months, with average family attendance of 30 weeks.

Philadelphia Society for Services to Children (Philadelphia Society)

Focusing on a high-risk, inner-city community, Philadelphia Society targeted its individual and group-based interventions to parents with children under the age of 6 years. The program offered a combination of center-based parent groups, a drop-in toy lending library, and a home-visiting component. Established as a replication of the Beethoven project in Chicago, Illinois, the home visitation model employed paraprofessional family advocates who focus on parental concerns and parent-child interaction during the biweekly visits. A family advocate and a community volunteer lead the parent groups, which used the Minnesota Early Learning Design model. This model consists of at least 2 years of biweekly group meetings emphasizing ways to enhance child development and parent-child interactions. The average parent participated in 26 weeks of service on a biweekly basis.

Youth Services, Inc. (YSI)

YSI targets its home-visiting and center-based educational services to pregnant and parenting teens in Philadelphia. Based on the work of David Olds and his colleagues (Olds, Henderson, Chamberlin, & Tatelbaum, 1986), the home visits were initiated during the mother's pregnancy and continued until the child reached 2 years of age. Trained paraprofessionals provide the home visits, with periodic visits by a nurse. YSI also offered center-based services three times a week. During the second funding cycle, the center-based education services were expanded to include a "Mother-Baby Movement Therapy" group that taught mothers how to interact with children in a developmentally beneficial way. Though the program was designed to serve families for 2 years, the typical participant enrolled for 50 weeks and participated in weekly services.

THE NCPCA EVALUATION

The conflicting information concerning the most effective child abuse prevention program strategies gleaned during the development of the Initiative led the William Penn Foundation to mandate that potential grantees agree to participate in an evaluation. The Foundation felt it was essential to identify the most effective mechanisms for working with high-risk families and to disseminate these findings to the field. To this end, the Foundation funded the NCPCA to create and implement a comprehensive evaluation strategy for this Initiative. NCPCA's Center on Child Abuse Prevention Research had considerable expertise in prevention research, especially in the areas of child welfare and comparative multisite program evaluation (Cohn, 1983; Daro, 1988; NCPCA, 1990).

The evaluation addressed three broad questions:

- How did the programs develop and evolve over time?

- Which interventions were most effective with which types of families?

- Were the programs' effects sustained over time?

The schema shown in Figure 1.1 guided our investigation.

The NCPCA study combined three related evaluation approaches: a process study, a client impact study, and a follow-up study. Although each strategy relied on different data sources and data collection techniques, each component served to inform the development of the next component. We outline each of these evaluation approaches in the following discussion. The intent is to provide readers with an understanding of the types of information used to develop our discussion of the practical guidelines for prevention program planning. For readers interested in a more technical discussion of the evaluation design, this information is provided in Resource A.

Process Study

Too often, program evaluators focus exclusively on participant outcomes without gaining a complete understanding of how prevention programs were designed and operated and how they changed over time. Before we designed our

14

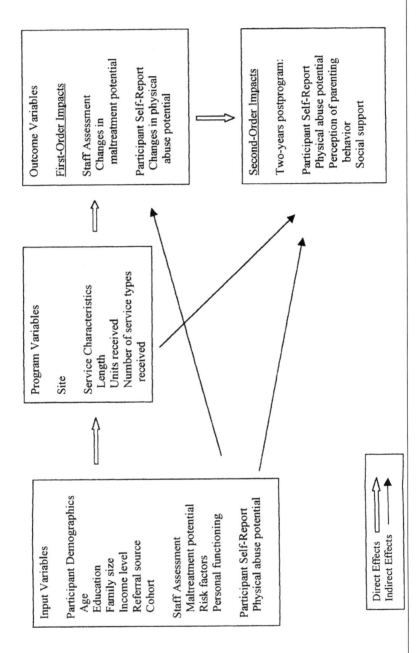

Figure 1.1. Conceptual Overview

Input Variables

Participant Demographics
Age
Education
Family size
Income level
Referral source
Cohort

Staff Assessment
Maltreatment potential
Risk factors
Personal functioning

Participant Self-Report
Physical abuse potential

Program Variables

Site

Service Characteristics
Length
Units received
Number of service types
received

Outcome Variables

First-Order Impacts

Staff Assessment
Changes in
maltreatment potential

Participant Self-Report
Changes in physical
abuse potential

Second-Order Impacts

Two-years postprogram:

Participant Self-Report
Physical abuse potential
Perception of parenting
behavior
Social support

Direct Effects
Indirect Effects

participant impact evaluation, we spent a lot of time collecting information about how the programs were formed, who they expected to serve, and how their services were structured. During the first year of the 5-year study, we developed detailed case studies for each of the nine sites based on observation of program services and in-depth interviews with project directors and supervisory and line staff. Each case study depicted the program's organizational structure; relationship to the host organization; child maltreatment prevention program goals; staff hiring and qualifications; training and supervisory procedures; participant recruitment strategies; intake procedures; the content, length, and frequency of each service component; and any follow-up procedures. To understand the community context of the programs, each case study also described the catchment area's particular economic and social conditions as well as the socioeconomic and demographic characteristics of the potential service population.

These initial case studies served as the building blocks for the remainder of our evaluation design. As we were interested in the continuing evolution of these programs, we continued over the subsequent 4 years to collect key program development data annually. Such information included any changes in participant population, staff composition, and program structure, as well as implementation issues. Aside from the value of documenting programmatic changes, information about each program's evolution often furthered our understanding of how the programs affected their participants over time.

Participant Impact Study

In keeping with our developmental evaluation approach, we designed the participant impact study component based on information drawn from the case studies developed during the study's first year. As shown in the previous program descriptions, we were faced with an almost unwieldy amount of variation in target population and service approaches. A key concern here was whether or not programs with such distinctively different interventions and target populations could be assessed by a single evaluation approach. At a minimum, we wanted to use a pretest and posttest assessment of families receiving services. However, this assumed that the same participants who started the programs would finish them as well. This was not always the case as some programs were designed to allow people to drop in as needed. Although the program staff may have wanted the same individuals to be involved over time, the voluntary nature of the programs did not require participants to follow a set case plan. A second barrier to implementing a pretest and posttest evaluation design was our assumption that service providers would conduct an "intake assessment" on the families they served. Again, the voluntary nature of these programs conflicted with this notion of an intake assessment, no matter how informal.

Although acknowledging the uniqueness of each program, we forged ahead with a single evaluation design to assess all the programs. Our thinking was that these differences could be useful in helping us understand what prevention strategies (or combinations) were most beneficial to what types of families.

Therefore, to look at the effectiveness of the nine programs, we relied on a quasi-experimental approach, with pretest and posttest assessment, in which the program sites act as comparisons for each other. We approached the analysis in two ways. First, we selected a program that offered the least amount of service, as measured by service duration and service contacts, as a "minimal service" comparison group. To go beyond this limited focus on one program as the comparison, our second strategy involved examining the relative impact of specific program characteristics on participant improvement, namely service intensity, service type, number of services offered, and service length.

The use of quasi-experimental designs in evaluation research is considered only moderately robust (Cook & Campbell, 1979), primarily because participants in the comparison group are not randomly assigned. The reason for random assignment is to ensure that participants who received the service possess the same demographic and risk characteristics as those with whom they are being compared. In our evaluation, we addressed this issue statistically. Because our sample size was larger than most program evaluation samples ($N = 490$), we were able to use multiple regression analysis, allowing us to statistically control for factors such as baseline variation that could conceivably account for differences in program impact (National Research Council, 1998). In essence, we equalized participant characteristics.

After deciding to use one evaluation approach to look at all the programs, choosing appropriate measures was the next hurdle. The study team reviewed all of the outcomes identified by the nine sites. Though stated differently, all of the programs identified improving parenting skills as a goal. Again looking back at the program goals, we considered a number of available standardized measures of parenting. Specifically, we were interested in how closely the measure reflected the program goals, ease of administration (as we knew the service providers would collect this information for us), and the established psychometric properties. In the end, we used two measures: the Child Abuse Potential Inventory (CAP; Milner, 1986) and a staff assessment protocol developed by NCPCA. Participants and staff completed both measures within the first 2 weeks of program entry and again at program termination.

CAP (Milner, 1986) measures a person's potential to engage in physical abuse, along with parental distress, rigidity, loneliness, problems with family, problems with child and self, and problems with others. We selected CAP over other potential measures for several reasons. First, it assessed parenting ability for parents with children in all age ranges. Our first-year case study showed that the programs were targeting parents with children of varying ages. Second, CAP has established risk categories based on overall scores. Individuals scoring 215 or more fall into the high-risk category, scores between 166 and 214 indicate moderate risk, and scores below 166 suggest a low potential for physical abuse (Milner, 1986). These established risk categories helped us understand the degree to which the programs reached their target population, the differences between how initially low-risk and high-risk parents fared in the prevention programs, and how participants changed over time.

Although CAP possesses strong psychometric properties (Milner, Gold, Ayoub, & Jacewitz, 1984; Milner, Gold, & Wimberly, 1986), a fact that evaluators value, program staff were reluctant to administer this instrument to parents with whom they were trying to establish a relationship. Some of the individual items on CAP are posed as deficit statements or appear intrusive.

Though the individual items are collapsed into a scale, program staff still tended to balk at the individual items. In particular, the tone of these items was diametrically opposed to their strength-based approach with families. We learned that the success of using CAP depended on how service providers presented it to the families. When service providers presented it as part of what they needed to do to ensure funding, families had no problems with completing the assessment. However, when service providers viewed it as an obstacle and an intrusion, families were more resistant. Indeed, one of the our greatest challenges to implementing the evaluation was convincing program staff to use CAP. Once the evaluation was completed, service providers were pleasantly surprised at how CAP could be used to answer critical programmatic issues.

The NCPCA staff assessment protocol was modified from an earlier instrument used to study several child abuse treatment programs (Daro, 1988). Based on unstructured interviews and observations, program staff recorded parents' demographic and economic information, assessed families on a checklist of 12 family risk factors and 10 adult functioning problems, and appraised the parent's likelihood to engage in seven forms of maltreating behavior: use of excessive corporal punishment; inadequate supervision; lack of emotional involvement; educational, physical, and emotional neglect; and failure to protect the child from abuse by others. (For more information on this measure, see McCurdy, 1995.)

Follow-Up Study

The final evaluation approach consisted of assessing participants' parenting attitudes and behaviors approximately 2 years after program termination. We conducted extensive, in-person interviews with 69 former participants regarding their recollections of how the programs helped them, their relationships with their service providers, and their current discipline strategies and interaction activities with their children. Current child-rearing practices were assessed in several ways. Parents were asked to respond to a number of age-specific child-rearing scenarios, followed by questions about their most recent discipline episode with each of their children. Using questions from a national public opinion poll on parenting (Daro, 1998), parents answered direct questions about their discipline techniques and attitudes toward child discipline. Last, we readministered CAP to the follow-up sample. The primarily qualitative approach used in this study component adds a dimension often overlooked in previous prevention program evaluations, the participants' voices.

ORGANIZATION OF THE BOOK

The information presented in this book seeks to advance our knowledge regarding the immediate and long-term impacts of child abuse prevention programs on parenting practices and attitudes. As described earlier, the nine sites offered a variety of interventions, varying in length and intensity. Likewise, the sample consisted of participants with varied racial, economic, and demographic characteristics. These two factors, in addition to the use of a multimethod research strategy, provide concrete results that programs can use to design or refine their current prevention and family support programming efforts. Furthermore, the heterogeneity of both the programs and service populations affords an excellent opportunity for addressing the crucial question: What prevention strategies work best for what families?

This book provides empirically derived information about improving the parenting skills of families experiencing numerous difficulties. As we intended to provide practical guidance to those in the family support field, each chapter ends with critical lessons learned, for three audiences: service providers, including planners, managers, and direct service staff; funders and policymakers, who are often one and the same; and researchers, especially those dedicated to prevention in all its forms. Our discussion is organized as follows. In the next chapter, we present the challenges the prevention programs faced as they implemented their programs. In Chapter 3, we discuss the immediate changes in parenting behaviors and attitudes related to program experience and specific program characteristics shown to improve parenting. Chapter 4 highlights the programs' impacts on long-term changes in parenting behaviors and attitudes. As changes in parenting do not occur in a vacuum, in Chapter 5, we describe internal and external barriers to parental change, focusing specifically on how parents met resistance from other family members and how parents cope with living in violent neighborhoods. As participant recruitment and retention posed difficulties for all of the programs, we devote chapter 6 to an in-depth discussion of some methods used to entice parents to enter the programs and to keep them involved. The final chapter summarizes how prevention programs can more effectively provide services to high-risk families.

CHAPTER 2

Program Implementation Challenges

In this book, we have applied a developmental approach not only to the families who chose to participate in the Initiative but to the programs themselves. Just as the parents modified their behavior and changed their parenting attitudes over time, the programs also refined and modified their service packages to meet the needs of the parents. Of some interest is the fact that the ecological paradigm of human development, with its acknowledgment that micro-, meso-, and macro-level factors influence an individual's growth (Belsky, 1984; Bronfenbrenner, 1979; Garbarino, 1990), nicely describes program development as well. As we will see, individual characteristics of the families (i.e., microsystem), the internal dynamics of the program, and the overall community setting (i.e., mesosystem) work together to foster or impede development for both parents and programs. In the case of the programs, the funding environment (e.g., macrosystem) also plays a key role in this maturation process.

Much of the published evaluation research on family support programs describes whether or not the program succeeded, that is, achieved a statistically significant impact on its participants. Though this emphasis on program effects is useful for determining which programs work, such studies often lack the descriptive detail that can be used by others to create programs able to achieve similar effects (Pietrzak, Ramler, Renner, Ford, & Gilbert, 1990). Furthermore, an exclusive focus on participant outcomes avoids the important developmental questions that planners and managers need answered to implement a worthwhile program, such as how the original program design took shape, the specifics of the service package, the internal and external forces that caused refinements to the overall model, and the methods successfully employed by the program to confront typical service barriers (e.g., high dropout rates). Because the Penn Initiative allowed the programs to design unique service packages with the overall goal of child abuse prevention, we had the opportunity to observe each program's evolution from conceptual design to viable intervention. Although the developmental trajectories of the nine programs varied, this chapter highlights the valuable lessons for future family support efforts that emerged from the common challenges faced and strategies employed by the Penn programs.

Program managers struggle with how to ensure a theoretical program model's being carried out on a daily basis. What may look highly promising on paper often can be difficult to achieve in the "real" world, even when the model has been successfully implemented elsewhere (Schorr, 1988; U.S. General Accounting Office, 1990), as was true for the subset of programs replicating other parenting interventions. Many times, a program's failure to achieve significant gains in parental functioning may be due to "low program integrity," the gap between the intended program design and its actual operation, rather than any weakness in the intervention model itself (Barnard, 1998; Davis & Savas, 1996).

To document the Penn programs' ability to deliver services as initially envisioned, we conducted an extensive process study throughout the 6-year evaluation period. Detailed profiles of each program were developed based on interviews with the following key informants during the first year of program operation: executive directors of the host agency; program directors; and all frontline staff, including volunteers (NCPCA, 1990). In addition, we reinterviewed the project directors annually regarding current implementation problems and changes in staffing patterns, participant characteristics, and program elements. These data were supplemented with information from program proposals and reports to identify the primary obstacles to program implementation and the most innovative methods used by the nine programs to overcome these barriers. The results help to illuminate the factors leading some programs to achieve success and others to struggle. As important, the findings offer insights into common pitfalls new family support programs may face and suggestions for avoiding these traps (Halpern, 1992).

No matter how thoroughly one plans for a new program, implementation barriers will inevitably arise just before or after service delivery begins, or both. For the most part, such barriers ensue when internal resources do not match external demands (Wandersman, 1982)—for instance, because the family's needs exceed the capacity of the service staff, the family drops out of the program. Though frustrating, encountering program obstacles represents a normal growing pain for any program and often leads to program refinements that enhance the quality of the service package. In this chapter, we consider the following forces that contribute to this developmental process: the types of families drawn to the program, the organization and structure of services, the community setting in which services take place, and the funding environment.

PARTICIPANT CHARACTERISTICS

The typical program designer devises a parenting program with a particular set of families in mind, be they first-time parents, at-risk families, or all families in a given community. When the family support program deliberately targets so-called at-risk or disadvantaged parents, as did these programs, we have found that planners and providers will encounter a spiraling level of familial risk over time. Families recruited to services at the 3-year point in a program's life often will look quite different than the types of families who enrolled during the first year. On the one hand, this process can be viewed as a sign of program success as more disadvantaged families take advantage of services. On the other hand, this process can create frustration for providers if the service design cannot meet this increased risk and if these higher-risk families tend to drop out of services, as is often the case. Program staff observed this phenomenon over the course of the Initiative as later families entered the programs with more chaotic lifestyles, characterized by frequent moves, changes in living conditions, and a higher portion of families living in shelters. Substance abuse issues also achieved more prominence over time. APM, for example, began serving more grandparents who had assumed responsibility for the care of their children's children, whereas Alternatives saw an increase in the number of active substance abusers in their programs.

Responsive programs often engage in a trial-and-error process to address such issues as they unfold (Goldberg, 1995). The experience of these programs illuminates two primary strategies for addressing the shifting needs of participants. First, the majority of programs responded to change in their participant population with programmatic innovations, ranging from minimal alterations, such as revising curricula, to radical restructuring through the addition or elimination of specific service components. An illustration of a minimal change occurred at FSA of Bucks County. As more families with substance abuse problems enrolled in services, FSA of Bucks County responded by introducing a segment on the relationship between substance abuse and child abuse to the Family Life Education series. This addition allowed FSA of Bucks County providers to raise the critical issue of drug use without significantly altering the service structure.

Other programs took a more aggressive approach when confronted with more chaotic family situations. For example, problems with housing led to high mobility for many of the families targeted by YSI. As a result, YSI encouraged staff to begin advocating for the clients with landlords, tenant action groups, and OSHA as a first step in providing services, instead of focusing on parent and child health issues as originally envisioned. This initial emphasis on satisfying personal needs has been found to be an effective retention method with higher-risk families (Lengua et al., 1992; Saylor, Elksnin, Farah, & Pope, 1990) and achieved success in this study as well. However, providers in family support programs need to be on their guard against losing sight of program goals altogether in the face of persistent family crises (Halpern, 1993; Halpern & Covey, 1983; Kitzman, Cole, Yoos, & Olds, 1997).

Offering some type of incentive to families was the second common method used to address increasing participant needs. As noted by Barth, Hacking, and Ash (1986), providing concrete goods and services attracted high-risk families to services. Most Penn programs relied on such enticements from the start, particularly in the forms of food and transportation. However, a few program managers instituted more innovative lures as higher-risk families entered services. For example, FSS initiated a day of respite child care each month for mothers with perfect attendance at their family school. YSI, faced with a highly mobile population that was hard to locate for home-based services, initiated a buddy system between active clients and more transitory families. The active clients helped to motivate and maintain contact with those who were having more trouble committing to continued participation in the program. Overall, these creative solutions helped solidify the involvement of multiproblem families.

PROGRAM ISSUES

Planning Process

Perhaps the most widespread reason for the emergence of implementation barriers is one that is most preventable: an inadequate planning process. Too often, insufficient time (Halpern, 1992) and resources have been allocated to this vital step, resulting in a flawed program design where services cannot be delivered as promised. The reasons for this are varied: Program managers may rush to provide services and shortchange this phase of program development (Halpern, 1992); funding agents may fail to recognize the importance of planning and allot minimal resources for this process; or the developers themselves may elect to forego this phase in the belief that the program is ready to go, especially if the "new" program replicates an existing service.

Curtailing the planning process usually leads to service delivery problems down the road for family support programs. For example, instead of conducting a community needs assessment, many of the Penn program proposals relied on published statistics concerning public health, housing patterns, and child maltreatment rates to estimate the service needs for families in the proposed service areas. Such data have their drawbacks. First, these global statistics often become outdated between the point of collection and time of publication. In the case of Philadelphia, the city continued to experience an economic decline along with an increase in the availability of illegal substances (Mitchel, 1990), with adverse impacts on the potential participants. Second, the data commonly collected by other agencies may not include the type of information necessary for program design, such as the resources and assets of the community or the community's perceptions of the most pressing problems. As a result, program planners can underestimate the level of risk in the target population, leading to overestimates of how many families the program can serve, especially in the first year of operation. The fact that a program does not meet the initial service estimates is often perceived as a failure in outreach or recruitment strategy, even though the fault resides in the initial planning process.

This planning weakness also has direct impacts on staffing plans. Program designers make decisions about the numbers, types, and qualifications of staff based on their knowledge of the current service environment. When this knowledge base is not derived from a comprehensive needs assessment, one can expect to find some major gaps between provider's abilities and participant needs. Similar to the experiences of family support programs involved in the Ford Foundation's Fair Start Initiative (Larner, Halpern, & Harkavy, 1992), most Penn program staffs were not fully equipped to handle the range of needs required by the families entering their programs. For example, staff at APM found that many of their Hispanic families could not benefit from parenting classes as they were illiterate in both Spanish and English. Furthermore, obtaining housing and food represented far more pressing needs than did receiving parent education. Even programs in the relatively advantaged suburban neighborhoods found that potential participants possessed fewer strengths than originally envisioned. Drug involvement by a family member, violence, inadequate housing, and poor education all competed with parenting concerns for the attention of the staff.

Methods to address planning gaps can take several forms. In the case of the Penn programs, the higher-than-expected risk profile forced revisions to proposed staffing plans to meet families' needs. For example, Alternatives opted to hire well-trained consultants instead of part-time staff because the applicant base for the part-time positions lacked the necessary qualifications. Others, such as FSS, felt compelled to hire more staff than initially expected, to address the presence of so many multiproblem families. In contrast, some programs (e.g., Crime Prevention) eliminated and revised positions due to low levels of initial response by families in the community. As this suggests, early recognition and flexibility are two keys for overcoming implementation obstacles.

The necessity for assessing community resources and needs may be even greater for family support programs hoping to use volunteers in the service provider role. Initially, several of the Penn programs incorporated the use of volunteers into their proposed staffing plans, with activities ranging from professionals delivering parenting workshops at FSS to community members assisting with a toy lending library at Philadelphia Society. Despite these intentions, efforts to recruit volunteers met with little success. Both community and professional volunteers were in short supply, suggesting to us that this type of resource may no longer be available to prevention programs, especially in disadvantaged neighborhoods. In fact, a couple of program directors explicitly stated that the use of volunteers was a middle-class concept that had no relevance in a very depressed, resource-poor community. To cover this manpower shortage, program managers either hired paid staff to provide the needed service, disbursed the responsibilities among the other service providers, or, if the position was tangential to the overall mission, eliminated the service entirely.

Program Location

For the most part, family support programs do not reside as stand-alone entities but instead operate within a broader service setting, such as a public health department, a social service agency, a hospital, or a child welfare agency. Though often overlooked as an essential component of the family support program, this "location" can constrain or enhance the program's eventual success. For example, a location within a well-known agency may facilitate the new program's integration into the community. However, this link can actually hinder a program's acceptance and growth if the host agency's goals substantially differ from those of the innovative program.

The experience of several Penn programs illustrated this latter point as the new programs' prevention focus clashed with the treatment orientation of the host agency. Several programs were housed in agencies that also provided Child Protective Services (CPS). Though this connection initially prompted a flow of referrals, the perception of the program as an extension of CPS resulted in referral sources sending families who had been reported for some type of maltreatment or who were currently engaged in maltreating behavior. As the Foundation's mandate precluded parents with CPS reports, the programs were then forced to expend efforts interviewing parents only to refer them to more appropriate services. In some instances, programs initially attempted to work with the maltreating families. As might be expected, such decisions divert energy away from recruiting and serving families who meet a program's criteria (Barth et al., 1986), thereby reducing, at least in the short term, the program's potential to fulfill its mission.

Some programs fell victim to Halpern's (1992) warning that "the agency's image colors the public perception of the program" (p. 196). Many eligible families perceived these new programs as associated with CPS due to the host agency's contract to provide some form of CPS service. Unexpectedly, this connection dampened initial recruitment efforts despite attempts by the prevention staff to establish a separate identity for the program. Though not universal, fear of CPS involvement emerged as a major force behind failure to recruit families into some programs, particularly at APM, a Hispanic, inner-city community, and in the ethnically mixed suburban area served by Alternatives of Pottstown.

Lack of Qualified Personnel

Of course, some implementation barriers are hard to avoid, no matter how thorough the initial design phase. Decisions about staff qualifications may be quite reasonable yet prove difficult to accomplish. Some Penn programs struggled to fill all of their paid staff positions because of the shortage of qualified counseling staff in the Philadelphia area, the relatively low salaries offered, and the nature of the work. Programs seeking qualified bilingual and bicultural staff encountered the most difficulties as few applicants were available. For family support programs offering home visitation services, program designers need to be aware that personal safety may emerge as a barrier to staff hiring, especially for programs that seek to employ nonindigenous visitors (Hiatt, Sampson, & Baird, 1997). In the current study, at least two programs grappled with finding social workers willing to make visits to the family's home due to safety fears. Again, awareness of the problem and a degree of flexibility in program design enabled most program managers to overcome these barriers. In fact, the experience of these programs demonstrates that staff recruitment issues will be a recurrent theme throughout a program's duration. Of all implementation barriers, however, problems in recruiting staff will be the most easily resolved without seriously compromising program integrity.

COMMUNITY SETTING

Just as family development is shaped by the community setting in which it occurs (Bronfenbrenner, 1979; Coulton, Korbin, Su, & Chow, 1995), program development also is subject to the forces exerted by the surrounding environment (Goldberg, 1995; Slaughter-Defoe, 1993). Three factors may be of particular relevance. First of all, a new family support program becomes a part of an existing network of community agencies. Whether this network welcomes the new program or eyes it with suspicion will partially determine eventual program success. As part of this integration process, the program must establish a referral network with these agencies, another area potentially fraught with tension. Articulating the mission, establishing realistic service estimates, and maintaining the commitment of referrers are some of the goals that can be a struggle to achieve. Last, program designers often fail to consider the cultural relevance or acceptability of the new service to the target families (Slaughter-Defoe, 1993), sometimes leading to that service element's failure.

Becoming Part of a Service Network

Achieving a recognized role in the local social service network can be a slow and turbulent process for new family support programs. In some instances, turf battles will arise between new programs and existing agencies. For example, FSS tried to enlist the help of a local church in referring families to the family school; however, the church viewed this program as competition with its own low-income day care center. Although the turf battles came as a surprise to the Penn programs, such competition for clients is not a rare event, especially in a community with scant social service resources, where agencies need to document a substantial client base. Confusion over the program's mission can also cause conflict with outside agencies. In the case of the Penn programs, "child abuse prevention" often meant preventing the recurrence of abuse in families, for the established network; however, in the terms of the Initiative, "prevention" was defined as enhancing parenting before any maltreatment transpired. As a result, staff at other agencies expected the new programs to accept anyone they recommended and oftentimes became frustrated when this didn't happen. We observed that joining and actively engaging in the community network and local task forces helped reduce this friction with local agencies. Such alliances serve to integrate the program into the community and reduce misperceptions regarding the program's intent. In fact, FSA of Bucks County was able to use the existing community network as its main referral source.

Referral Sources

Although the referral process receives little mention in most evaluation studies, the establishment of an effective referral network is a vital first step for a successful program (Barth et al., 1986). The experience of these and other family support programs revealed that the hurdles in getting these networks off the ground usually came in one of two forms. First, a decision to rely on the host agency's existing referral networks usually carries a hidden cost. On the positive side, this network typically responds with an immediate flow of referrals for families potentially in need of services. Unfortunately, many of these families do not meet the new program's eligibility criteria. Often, existing service agencies view the new program as a place to send families they have not been successful with or are unable to serve rather than referring families who meet the new program's intake criteria. The limited availability of supportive or treatment services in the Philadelphia area meant that many of the families initially referred to the Penn programs suffered from severe problems, such as active substance abuse, mental illness, and domestic violence, even though most programs clearly indicated that families with this level of dysfunction could not be served through their prevention services. Program managers found themselves in a quandary—to accept all comers or to stick with the original recruitment criteria. For the most part, managers decided to accept as many families as possible. We would recommend against this path as these programs later faced the serious problem of inadequate staffing and service options to effectively address the needs of these multiproblem families.

In the second scenario, new programs decide to establish an independent referral network only to be surprised by the slow trickle of referrals in the initial months of program operation. The hurdle for these types of programs is overcoming the common misperception that parents will come flocking to services once the program doors open. In the words of Barth et al. (1986, p. 104), "Child abuse prevention programs often seem like a good idea to everyone except high-risk mothers." The experience of the Penn program managers reflected this common service barrier. Without an established community presence, these programs initially recruited fewer families than promised in their grant proposals and had a hard time gaining the acceptance and trust of established community agencies, local churches, and schools.

In the long run, however, perseverance pays off. For example, both Crime Prevention and YSI engaged in aggressive community outreach activities through flyers, local advertising, frequent presentations to community agencies, and door-to-door canvassing of neighborhoods. Though the two programs did not initially attract large numbers of families, these time-consuming efforts eventually brought in the types of families whose problems could be addressed and who would participate in the parenting programs. The fact that word-of-mouth referrals increased and recruitment problems were more quickly resolved with these methods are two primary benefits of this approach.

A unique problem for some programs concerned dependence on one primary referral source. In the course of the Initiative, the connection between this primary referral source and the prevention program often broke down. FSS, for example, had cultivated a close relationship with the social work staff at a nearby hospital that provided the bulk of referrals to the program. Significant turnover among the staff in this department, however, disrupted the flow of referrals and caused FSS to question their reliance on hospital referrals. Similarly, Philadelphia Society anticipated the help of a local church in referring prospective families. When the head of the church took another position, however, the new minister did not follow through with referrals, forcing the staff at Philadelphia Society to devise new recruitment strategies.

We urge family support programs to avoid this single-source recruitment strategy and, instead, actively engage a number of referral sources as this will facilitate the program's integration into the community. Furthermore, programs can reduce potential disruption in their referral networks by broadening recruitment strategies to include direct outreach methods. This technique gives program staff greater control over the client engagement process, thereby allowing them to reach the types of families the program had targeted. Direct outreach also increases the visibility of the program in the community. For example, both Alternatives and FSA of Bucks County began conducting outreach at a homeless shelter, and Crime Prevention presented workshops to prospective clients at a domestic violence shelter. The most unusual example of direct outreach may be the decision of YSI to start conducting outreach for teen parents in a neighborhood shopping mall where many of the community's teenagers spent their free time. Overall, successful networks will be achieved by educating potential referral sources prior to program implementation, developing and following a comprehensive outreach plan, and revisiting and refining network collaborations throughout the program's life (Barth et al., 1986).

Cultural Relevance

Programs offering a variety of service components often struggle to get at least one service element off the ground. The experience of the Penn programs leads us to believe that some elements fail because they do not correspond to the cultural or community norms of the target participants. For example, staff at APM attributed their difficulties with attracting Hispanic families to the center-based support group to cultural concerns over privacy issues. Parents at FSP attended the education groups but avoided the counseling component, as they viewed receipt of counseling as an indicator of problems or a stigma. Home visitation proved much less attractive than center-based services for the African American parents participating in the program at FSS.

As our data did not address whether cultural, familial, or financial barriers caused the failure of specific program elements, it remains an area in need of further research. For now, we recommend that, as part of an initial community needs assessment, programs should assess the acceptability of specific services to the families they wish to serve and devise service strategies that do not conflict with the prevailing cultural norms in that community (Slaughter-Defoe, 1993).

FUNDING ENVIRONMENT

Although the funding environment is a part of the community setting, we discuss this separately due to its salience for program planners and managers.

Funding issues exert a prominent influence on programmatic decision making. As such, the experiences of the Penn programs offer several examples of barriers and corresponding changes caused by funding concerns.

Efforts to secure and maintain adequate resources present an ongoing struggle for program managers, with spillover effects on staff and participants alike. Though these programs were successful in acquiring the initial 3-year grant from the Penn Foundation, most encountered a common pitfall when searching for continuation funds: Potential funding sources prefer to fund new or pilot programs as opposed to already established family support services. As noted by Goldberg (1995), managers facing this situation must expend valuable time seeking new resources while providers work in an atmosphere of uncertainty and low morale, often with negative effects on service delivery. Most of the Penn program managers were unable to secure new resources for their programs; fortunately, about 1 month after the original funding period ended, the Penn Foundation decided to refund nine of the original 14 programs for an additional 3-year cycle. Though this allowed services to continue, most programs lost key staff during the transition period. Loss of staff dissuaded some families from further service involvement and forced the closure or curtailment of some service elements.

Program planners and funders can fall into the trap of thinking that "more is better." When planners develop service proposals, there can be pressure to make overly optimistic claims about the number of families that will be served by the new program. This is probably a response to the perception that funders are more likely to give grants to programs that can reach a substantial target audience in a given year. Unfortunately, this emphasis on size may come at the expense of the program's quality (Barth et al., 1986). Furthermore, the program's promise to serve large numbers may initially attract the grant but lead to later problems with the funder if that program cannot meet the original service population estimates. For some of the original 14 programs funded by the Penn Foundation, this failure directly resulted in the Foundation's decision to forego refunding that specific program after the first 3-year grant period ended.

Last, Goldberg (1995) reminds us that the funder's goals may conflict with the goals and priorities of the social program. In the case of the Penn programs, one funding caveat caused friction for some programs. As part of the funding contract, programs had to agree to participate in an outcome evaluation conducted by an outside evaluator. In this way, the Foundation staff could assess the effectiveness of their investment. Programs with previous evaluation experience did not perceive this requirement as burdensome; these managers believed that the immediate stress of an outside entity monitoring the program could be offset by the future value of a positive evaluation for securing additional funds. Programs without this experience had more misgivings about the evaluation process. As one might expect, both frontline staff and managers expressed concerns that valuable time would be spent completing evaluation protocols instead of serving at-risk families. Though program managers were more likely to understand the long-term benefits of an evaluation than frontline providers, maintaining staff commitment to this process required ongoing interface between the evaluators and service providers. Overall, program staff were quite responsive to the demands of the evaluation, but better preparation by the Foundation and the research team would have helped smooth this road.

LESSONS LEARNED

As we have seen, most new family support programs can expect to implement programmatic refinements to address the implementation barriers that are part and parcel of service provision. For the most part, such alterations represent a normal and healthy evolution for prevention programs of this nature (Halpern, 1992). Indeed, program planners should anticipate both minor and major tinkering with specific program elements for as long as the program operates. However, programs must beware of losing sight of original goals and mission when trying to meet the needs of all families asking for assistance (Barth et al., 1986).

The experience of Alternatives epitomizes this last consideration. Over the course of the Initiative, Alternatives added services for special-needs children, off-site parent groups for clients unable to come to the center, individual counseling offered at subsidized housing projects, an additional parent-child play group for older children, and off-site educational workshops. The end result was a hodgepodge of services lacking a coherent design and focus. Staff found themselves stretched and facing increased conflict with host organizations over the goals and responsibilities of the program. This scenario highlights the importance of managed change versus program drift (Pecora, Haapala, & Fraser, 1991). *Program drift,* defined as change occurring in bits and pieces, lacking a coherent direction or agenda, can undermine a program's foundations and weaken its impact. In contrast, managed change, or change that is grounded in program theory, objectives, and research, will most likely advance the program's ability to effectively assist families.

Though examining the evolution of a family support initiative may not be as glamorous as demonstrating program efficacy, it is a critical first step for understanding how to best enhance family functioning through societal interventions. The collective story of these nine programs highlights some valuable lessons that emerged over the course of the Initiative, lessons that not only helped these programs grow and mature but that also have meaning for anyone interested in the dynamic process of program development. In this section, we present some of the key conclusions we have drawn from this process study, our own evaluation experience with other parenting efforts, and the limited program development research available from the family support field.

Service Providers

- As should be evident, the critical first step for any program designer is to conduct a thorough needs assessment to determine the goodness of fit between the proposed service, needs of the target population, current service environment, proposed staff qualifications, and the incentives for program involvement.

- A key voice that should be heard in this planning process is that of the potential program participants (Goldberg, 1995). Although few family support programs involve the target audience during the planning stage, we believe that laying this groundwork will promote more culturally relevant and compatible services and ensure a solid match between program goals and participant needs, thereby avoiding the problems of service underuse and participant attrition experienced by most new programs.

- We endorse the input evaluation model advocated by Pietrzak et al. (1990). This model recognizes that families, programs, and communities are not stagnant; instead, planners and managers need to routinely update and incorporate needs assessment data into the program design process to ensure a consistent and high-quality service.

- To monitor service delivery, recognize potential barriers as quickly as possible, and maintain a high service standard, programs should develop a management information system to provide continuous feedback into the ongoing program development process (Goldberg, 1995). If at all possible, this system should be integrated with any outcome evaluation in process.

- Regardless of outreach method, program developers should anticipate devoting from 3 to 6 months to refining the initial recruitment process. Though it may be that the Philadelphia situation was unique in terms of participant risk and lack of alternative services for eligible families, inserting a new family support program into an at-risk community appears to require substantial efforts in terms of articulating what such programs can and cannot do and gaining trust from established community groups and residents.

Funders and Policymakers

- If funding agents truly wish to aid in generating effective intervention strategies to improve the lives of children and their families, resources must be allocated for program planners to conduct comprehensive community assessments, even when the planner will be replicating an established service. As noted here and in other studies, the context in which the program operates can influence every aspect of program functioning (Halpern, 1992). Without such information prior to program implementation, many family support efforts will encounter the service barriers described here and will struggle to achieve their desired program goals.

- When making funding decisions, we advocate that funders place greater emphasis on the quality of the service rather than the number of families served (Barth et al., 1986). Both families and communities will reap more benefits from small but effective service delivery designs than from prevention approaches that provide minimal services to as many people as possible.

- Funders should require and financially support independent process and outcome evaluations as part of the grant process. In this regard, the William Penn Foundation exemplified a "best practice" standard by including an evaluation provision in the RFP and by directly funding a comprehensive evaluation. Furthermore, the regular grant review process should incorporate standards that promote the integration of data collection and evaluation findings into the individual development process for each program.

- Although we acknowledge the importance of outcome evaluations, one of the primary lessons learned from this and other new family support initiatives (Halpern, 1992) is that transforming an original proposal into a smoothly running program takes at least 1 year. For this reason, we recommend that funders require outcome evaluations to begin in the second year of service delivery. Data collection, however, should be integrated into routine program management at the onset of the grant.

- Our most critical recommendation concerns the urgent need for funding agents to reconsider the current emphasis on providing seed money or start-up funds and instead, provide consistent funding to existing family support programs (Schorr, 1988; U.S. General Accounting Office, 1990).

- As is often the case, the Penn programs had great difficulty locating new funding streams at the end of the first 3-year grant period due to funders' reluctance to support ongoing services. The Penn Foundation's decision to continue supporting these programs represents a solid commitment to families that will achieve more lasting effects than short-term demonstration projects, no matter how thorough or well-financed the projects.

- Policymakers can assist in creating an overall service environment that is conducive to quality program design and implementation by converting from the dominant short-term perspective, that emphasizes immediate noteworthy outcomes in relatively brief time frames (U.S. General Accounting Office, 1990), to a long-term vision that equally supports process and outcome studies along with sustained funding for family support programs.

- Policies should favor community-based approaches that incorporate the following standards: Programs should be tailored to the needs of the residents, reflective of neighborhood resources and voids, and open to some degree of program flexibility in response to emerging issues and trends.

- The emphasis on replicating so-called proven family support programs needs to be rethought in light of the importance of contextual factors. The target participants, program staff and structure, and surrounding neighborhood environment will all influence the actual delivery of services, making it unlikely that one standard service model can consistently achieve positive effects in a variety of settings.

Researchers

- The scant information on the methods by which programs successfully recognize and respond to implementation barriers strongly indicates the need for studies that explicitly examine these issues. By investigating and reporting on these challenges, researchers can help program developers and managers overcome or avoid barriers that often lead to a program's downfall.

- We strongly urge that researchers incorporate ecological designs in the evaluation process. With such methods, we can begin to understand how contextual factors influence program design and delivery, thereby enhancing our ability to develop effective family support programs. Such methods would integrate both process and outcome data; use information from a variety of sources, including participants, service staff, community actors, and funders; and focus on the relationships between these groups to explain outcomes.

- Program staff needs to become partners in the evaluation process. To this end, researchers should include program staff in the evaluation design stage, if at all possible, and solicit staff input throughout the evaluation process. Aside from helping to ensure that providers support and understand the evaluation process, collaborating with program staff provides an opportunity to create a formal system that feeds research results into the program development process, a vital step for enhancing service quality and success.

CHAPTER **3**

Changes in Parenting Practices

No one strategy for preventing child abuse had been identified as the most promising at the time the William Penn Foundation decided to invest its resources in child abuse prevention. During the course of the Child Abuse Prevention Initiative, studies evaluating the efficacy of family support programs mushroomed (Fink & McCloskey, 1990; Health Care Coalition on Violence, 1998; Olds & Kitzman, 1993; U.S. General Accounting Office, 1990), yet few compared the relative strengths and weaknesses of different approaches to prevention (Wekerle & Wolfe, 1993). In fact, a number of other vital questions remain unanswered, including whether certain types of programs produce greater benefits for some types of families (Daro & McCurdy, 1994) or what amount of services are needed to change parenting behavior (Guterman, 1997; Daro & McCurdy, 1994). The diversity across the nine Penn programs in terms of service structure and participant characteristics allowed us to begin addressing these key questions. In this chapter, we discuss the short-term impacts of the Initiative in the context of these overarching questions. As will be shown, the method through which the family entered the program and the frequency of contact with program staff directly correspond to who benefits from prevention services. In addition, our findings regarding relative program effectiveness led us to propose some hypotheses regarding the connections between a program's success, its structure, and characteristics of the family. We argue that the parent's developmental needs and resources must inform the service delivery process (Berlin, O'Neal, & Brooks-Gunn, 1998), suggesting that programs need to craft individualized approaches for each family.

In designing this study, we hoped not only to assess the relative effectiveness of the nine programs but also to address two other issues of interest to the family support field. First, prevention advocates, as a group, have long struggled with the dilemma of how to best serve families at all points along the risk continuum (Guterman, 1997). Some would advocate that families falling into the high-risk spectrum cannot be helped through voluntary prevention services because they require intensive therapeutic interventions. As attempts to recruit and retain more disadvantaged families represent a fundamental stumbling block for many secondary prevention programs (McCurdy, Hurvis, & Clark, 1996), the empirical research base has not been able to tell us whether such families can be helped through family support services. The success of these nine programs in enrolling high-risk parents provided the opportunity to revisit this issue and investigate what services promote parenting improvements among the most vulnerable families.

Second, concern exists over whether prevention services are designed to match the parenting norms or practices of the cultural group targeted for the intervention (Slaughter-Defoe, 1993). Too often, a program designed in one cultural context is applied to another without any regard for important familial or ecological differences that may impede service delivery. Along with this issue of cultural compatibility between service type and target population is the failure of program evaluations to examine how impacts vary within cultural groups and whether certain service characteristics are more likely to produce the expected outcomes in some subpopulations but not others (Pumariega, 1996). As a first look at this issue, we investigate whether any one service type appeared to be more effective among programs serving African American neighborhoods. Such information is vital for designing and implementing truly supportive services across and within diverse cultural groups.

MEASURES

After consulting with providers at each program, we chose two measures to assess how parenting and the child-rearing environment changed over the course of these interventions. Program staff completed an appraisal of the parent's likelihood to engage in seven forms of maltreating behavior: use of excessive corporal punishment; inadequate supervision; lack of emotional involvement; educational, physical, and medical neglect; and failure to protect the child from abuse by others. We also obtained the parents' self-reports of change in punitive child-rearing attitudes as measured by the Child Abuse Potential Inventory (CAP; Milner, 1986). CAP assesses one's potential to engage in physical child abuse along with parental distress, rigidity, loneliness, problems with family, problems with child and self, and problems with others. Extensive analyses have identified three established risk categories based on overall scores, with individuals scoring 215 or more falling into the high-risk category, scores between 166 and 214 indicating moderate risk, and scores below 166 suggesting a low potential for physical abuse (Milner, 1986).

These measures provide two distinct views of program impacts and, in the case of corporal punishment, allow us to compare the perspective of the parent to that of the staff. Unfortunately, we were not able to supplement these perspectives with other types of data, such as official reports of child maltreatment from CPS or clinical observations of parent-child interactions. State child abuse data often are considered to be the primary indicator of successful prevention efforts, especially by state legislators, policymakers, and funders. However, our experience with CPS data has convinced us that the numerous flaws and potential biases (see Daro, 1991; McCurdy, 1996) associated with most state CPS systems argue against their use if one wishes to obtain an accurate appraisal of family functioning. For example, a national study found that one third of child maltreatment incidents go unreported (Sedlak & Broadhurst, 1996), so reliance on this data will produce an incomplete picture. Observing the interactions between a parent and child typically provides a better picture of the parent-child relationship than maltreatment reports, as a trained clinician can assess qualities beyond abusive behavior, such as the level of maternal warmth, sensitivity, and nurturing offered to the child (Wolfe, 1991); however, financial considerations often prohibit the use of this approach, as was true in this study.

At this juncture, a few limitations of the measures must be noted before we can discuss the findings. In assessing the data's reliability, we found that staff assessments of potential for maltreating behaviors showed great variability across programs and relatively low correspondence with the participant's self-report measure of physical child abuse potential. Such low interrater reliability levels among the program staff limited the comparability of the staff assessments. As will be discussed, staff at many of the programs appeared to be reluctant to categorize these parents as likely to engage in any maltreating behaviors despite the extreme CAP scores posted by half of our sample. This discrepancy caused us to put limited faith in the staff assessments. Instead, we relied primarily on changes in CAP scores to determine program impact. However, as the programs sought to address more than just physical abuse potential, we present the results from the staff assessment instrument as a preliminary indicator of these other outcomes.

FAMILY PROFILES

One of the most promising and, in some ways, surprising findings from our study was the success these programs enjoyed in recruiting so-called at-risk parents. Over the course of 5 years, the nine programs enrolled 840 parents from the Greater Philadelphia area. Table 3.1 shows the types of difficulties these fami-

TABLE 3.1 Demographic Characteristics of Program Participants (by percentage)

Characteristics	Alternatives (n = 42)	APM (n = 61)	Congreso (n = 150)	Crime Prevention (n = 119)	FSA of Bucks County (n = 130)	FSP (n = 30)	FSS (n = 104)	Philadelphia Society (n = 78)	YSI (n = 126)	Total (n = 840)
Sex										
Male	2.4	0.0	4.0	7.6	20.8	10.0	4.8	1.3	16.7	8.7
Female	97.6	100.0	96.6	90.8	79.2	90.9	94.2	98.7	81.0	90.6
Missing	0.0	0.0	0.0	1.7	0.0	0.0	1.0	0.0	2.4	0.7
Race										
American Indian	0.0	0.0	0.7	0.0	0.0	0.0	0.0	0.0	0.8	0.2
Asian	0.0	0.0	0.7	0.0	1.5	0.0	2.9	2.6	0.8	1.1
African American	26.2	1.6	12.0	90.8	10.0	96.7	89.4	88.5	89.7	54.2
Hispanic	4.8	95.1	82.7	7.6	1.5	0.0	1.0	2.6	0.8	23.7
White	66.7	1.6	4.0	0.8	86.2	0.0	2.9	3.8	0.8	18.5
Other	2.4	0.0	0.0	0.8	0.8	3.3	2.9	2.6	5.6	1.9
Missing	0.0	1.6	0.0	0.0	0.0	0.0	1.0	0.0	1.6	0.5
Marital status										
Married	21.4	34.4	19.3	14.3	50.8	10.0	15.4	5.1	0.8	19.8
Separated	16.7	27.9	9.3	18.5	20.8	3.3	7.7	3.8	0.8	11.9
Divorced	0.0	8.2	5.3	5.9	12.3	3.3	2.9	0.0	0.0	4.8
Widowed	2.4	1.6	0.7	1.7	0.8	0.0	1.0	2.6	0.0	1.1
Never married	59.5	18.0	56.0	48.7	9.2	53.3	59.6	88.5	92.1	53.9
Missing	0.0	9.8	9.3	10.9	7.7	30.3	13.5	0.0	6.4	8.1
Income										
Less than $15,000	57.1	82.0	68.0	61.3	33.8	76.7	55.8	65.4	69.8	61.1
$15,000 to $24,999	16.7	9.8	4.0	21.8	26.2	6.7	10.6	11.5	14.3	14.2

	Mean	Mean	Mean	Mean	Mean	Mean	Mean	Mean	Mean	Mean
$25,000 plus	9.5	0.0	0.7	2.5	36.9	3.3	1.9	0.0	2.4	7.4
Missing	16.7	8.2	27.4	14.2	3.1	13.3	31.8	23.1	13.5	17.4
Public assistance										
Yes	69.0	95.1	61.3	79.8	34.6	76.7	82.7	84.6	83.3	71.3
No	31.0	3.3	20.7	12.6	59.2	13.3	3.5	12.8	8.7	21.1
Missing	0.0	1.6	18.0	7.6	7.8	10.0	3.8	2.6	9.0	7.6
Employment										
Employed	14.3	1.6	14.7	26.1	58.5	13.3	9.6	7.7	7.9	19.8
Not employed	85.7	98.4	84.0	71.4	40.8	86.7	90.4	91.0	91.3	79.3
Missing	0.0	0.0	1.3	2.5	0.8	0.0	0.0	1.3	0.8	0.9
Education										
Less than high school	50.0	70.5	63.3	29.4	14.6	33.3	41.3	61.5	76.2	48.8
High school graduate	16.7	16.4	28.0	52.1	52.3	30.0	32.7	24.4	16.7	32.4
Post high school	19.0	9.8	6.7	9.2	25.4	16.7	15.4	6.4	6.3	12.1
Missing	14.3	3.3	2.0	9.2	7.7	20.0	10.6	7.7	0.8	6.7
	Mean	Mean	Mean	Mean	Mean	Mean	Mean	Mean	Mean	Mean
Age	22.7	33.9	26.4	31.5	33.5	30.6	26.1	22.4	19.2	27.3
Number of Children	1.0	3.1	2.0	2.3	2.2	2.5	2.1	2.2	1.6	2.1

All comparisons are significant ($p < .05$).

lies endured. For example, one marker of distress—economic deprivation—was pervasive. Almost two thirds of the parents were attempting to raise two or more children with incomes of less than $15,000 per year. In fact, close to three quarters received some type of public assistance. Studies have exposed the negative consequences of economic hardship on parenting in terms of risk for maltreatment (Elder, Liker, & Cross, 1984; Gelles, 1989), suggesting that many of these children were living in potentially harmful environments.

According to data on household structure, most parents did not receive emotional or financial support for child rearing in their own home, potentially limiting their capacity to supply consistent quality care for their children (Bradley et al., 1994; McLoyd, 1990; National Research Council, 1993). Single parenthood was the norm (54%) with only 20% of parents married at the time they enrolled in services. The fact that these parents averaged 27 years of age and had two biological children living with them suggests that the typical participant had already garnered some experience in her parenting role at the time she sought out support services. As a group, the participants had racially diverse backgrounds, with 54% African American, 24% Hispanic, and 19% white.

As shown in Table 3.1, we found some notable demographic distinctions among the program participants. For example, FSA of Bucks County and YSI were the only two sites to serve a substantial portion of male participants. In the case of FSA of Bucks County, these men attended services with their wives. At YSI, however, a separate group was created for fathers. On average, parents at APM were older (i.e., 34) and had more children than those from the other eight programs, though Crime Prevention, FSA of Bucks County, and FSP also worked with older participants. In contrast, YSI attracted the youngest parents, averaging 19 years of age. Staff at Alternatives worked with the most ethnically mixed population; the remaining programs generally served one ethnic group, reflecting the community's makeup.

Table 3.2 describes how the service provider viewed these families. Overall, providers observed a fairly high number of risk factors and adult functioning problems when families entered services. Social isolation, often linked to neglectful and punitive parenting behavior (see Garbarino & Sherman, 1980; Thompson, 1995), appeared to be rampant among these parents. Close to half were assessed as isolated from friends and family and living in communities with scarce resources or limited support systems. One third of the parents had grown up in households where discipline typically involved physical punishment, which increased the likelihood that these parents would rely on similar disciplinary tactics with their own children (Gelles & Straus, 1988). Another third experienced difficulties with child care, or were trying to adapt to the presence of an infant, or both, at the time they enrolled. Indeed, only 16% of these families were rated as not exhibiting any of the 12 risk factors at the start of services.

TABLE 3.2 Frequency of Risk Factors[a] and Adult Functioning Problems[b] (by percentage)

Risk Factors	Present	Adult Functioning Problems	Mild	Severe
Social isolation	47.7	Lack of child development knowledge	62.7	19.3
Few community resources	44.6	Inaccurate understanding of child's behavior	61.2	16.7
History of physical discipline	32.6	Inaccurate sense of child's needs	51.9	17.6
Difficulties with child care	30.6	Excessive need for compliance	49.9	13.6
Pregnancy, new baby	29.8	Unable to manage stress	45.7	20.8
Ambivalence about parenthood	27.7	Expects emotional support from child	45.5	10.7
Substance abuse	22.3	Low self-esteem	44.5	23.2
Household violence	14.9	Inability to manage anger appropriately	43.8	20.8
Partner change	14.0	Neglects family duties	31.2	11.5
Death, medical crisis	13.2	Lack of interest in child	25.6	8.5
Inconsistent prenatal care	9.4			
Children in placement	8.6			

a. $N = 829$ due to the exclusion of 11 respondents with missing data on more than 50% of the risk factors.
b. $N = 831$ due to the exclusion of 9 respondents with missing data on more than 50% of the adult functioning problems.

Providers were more apt to note personal functioning problems than familial risk factors among their families. The most prevalent of these problems included lack of child development knowledge, inappropriate interpretation of the child's behavior, inaccurate sense of the child's needs, and an excessive need for the child to comply with parental wishes. Such difficulties have long been thought to heighten parental stress and the likelihood of harsh parenting behavior (Browne & Saqi, 1988). Although not as prevalent, low self-esteem and inability to appropriately manage anger or stress represented the most severe functioning problems for the group. In fact, only 7% were judged as presenting no adult functioning problems at service intake.

We were not surprised to learn that program staff assessed participants as having more adult functioning problems than risk factors. Parents generally sought out these programs to address a specific problem, be it a parenting concern, a need for resources, or a desire to reduce social isolation, and therefore tended to share these pressing concerns with staff at the program's start. In contrast, parents were less likely to volunteer to staff that they enrolled to address a chronic source of risk, such as physical violence in the household or substance abuse, though staff often became aware of these problems over the course of the intervention.

Staff ratings of a parent's likelihood to engage in a broad range of maltreating behaviors suggested that most participants (75%) were viewed as unlikely to harm a child in any of these ways. However, some distinctions emerged among those found to have some maltreatment potential. For example, staff rated over 20% of the participants as likely to display at least one of the following behaviors toward their children: excessive use of corporal punishment (26%), lack of emotional involvement (26%), and inadequate supervision (22%). Less than 14% were assessed as likely to neglect their child's physical, medical, or educational needs or to fail to protect the child from abuse by others.

Despite these low maltreatment ratings by staff, participant scores on the CAP indicated a substantial risk for physical child abuse. The average initial CAP score of 219 ($SD = 105$) for the 746 participants with complete data places these parents in the highest risk category for physical abuse potential, a level reached by only 5% of a comparison group of parents studied by Milner (1986). In fact, half of the sample posted initial CAP scores in this high-risk category, twice the number judged by staff to be even somewhat likely to use excessive corporal punishment.

We were intrigued by the contrasting profiles that emerged from the staff's assessments of the participants. For the most part, parents were viewed as living in risky environments and demonstrating substantial dysfunction yet evidencing a low propensity for child maltreatment. This discrepancy raises some questions about the accuracy of these ratings as most research would suggest a close link between risk factors and abuse potential (Ayoub, Jacewitz, Gold, & Milner, 1983; Milner, 1986). Indeed, an earlier study with this same population found that parents with more punitive parenting attitudes were judged by staff as having more functioning problems and risk factors (McCurdy, 1995). In addition, anecdotal information conveyed the impression that staff thought they were serving very high-risk parents.

Though we were puzzled by this discrepancy, at least two explanations come to mind. First, the providers may have been reluctant to label families as potentially abusive to avoid losing a parent's trust and cooperation. Our evidence suggests that this may be especially true for paraprofessionals who often wish to help families avoid the stigma that can be associated with social service involvement. We found that staff at Philadelphia Society, which employed the most paraprofessionals, were the least likely to rate any parent as potentially abusive. A second possibility was that the staff could not make accurate assessments of child abuse potential at the start of services. It is quite likely that providers need to be engaged with the family before they can understand the internal family dynamics that may put children at risk. In this study, most providers had had only two or three contacts with the parent at the time they completed these assessments, a brief period for making sensitive judgments. Staff ratings may therefore reflect the provider's limited knowledge of the family.

Although the exact explanation is unknown, this inconsistency suggests that evaluators should be cautious when documenting baseline risk for maltreatment and avoid relying solely on initial staff impressions.

As shown by these family profiles, the nine prevention programs succeeded to a large degree at their efforts to enroll high-risk families. The considerable amounts of financial stress, social isolation, and potential for physical abuse that characterized most families illustrate the programs' ability to attract extremely disadvantaged parents in the most vulnerable Philadelphia neighborhoods. Perhaps more important, this success tells us that despite their dismal economic and living conditions, many parents are concerned enough about their children's well-being to seek out ways to improve their parenting skills. When the opportunity to find help with their child-rearing or personal issues arose, such parents took the initiative to enroll in voluntary services.

CHANGES IN PARENTING CAPABILITIES

The ability of the Penn Prevention Initiative to successfully enroll and maintain a large portion of disadvantaged families in some of the highest-risk neighborhoods in Philadelphia afforded the opportunity to explore the utility of prevention services with a traditionally underserved and unexamined population (Wolfe, 1991). As recounted by parents in the interview data presented in the following chapters, many of the mothers grew up in extremely neglectful or abusive households yet they still strove to create a better environment for their children. The data we present here indicate that prevention efforts can make a difference in the struggle to become better parents, even for those facing enormous internal and external obstacles to nurturing.

The Typical Participant

Our first look at changes in parental attitudes toward child rearing, using the CAP, suggested remarkable improvements between the time parents enrolled and left services. Overall, 490 parents (58%) completed the CAP at both time points. As no substantive differences between the initial characteristics of completing mothers and those in the total sample ($n = 840$) were found, we have some assurance that the findings may be generalized to the full complement of participants. According to the parent's self-report of physical abuse potential, these parents significantly ($p < .001$) reduced their average CAP scores by 16 points or 8% of their initial CAP scores. In fact, Figure 3.1 reveals that the aver-

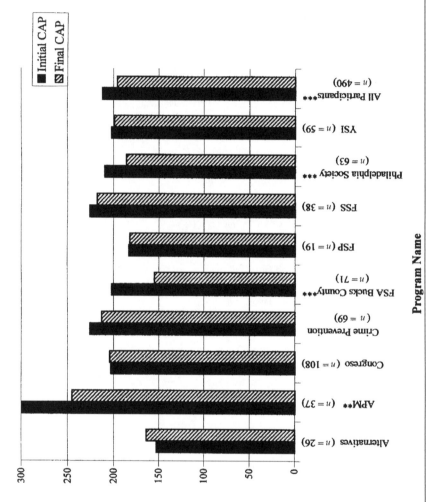

Figure 3.1. Change in CAP Scores for All Participants

N = 490; *p* < .05; **p* < .01; ***p* < .001.

44

age parent at seven of the nine programs substantially reduced her child abuse potential over the course of services.

Taken at face value, however, these figures are potentially misleading. For instance, scores may have improved because parents became familiar with CAP and gave more socially acceptable answers the second time around, though CAP includes several lie and validity scales to help guard against this type of occurrence (see Milner, 1986). And we found a high correlation between initial and final scores ($r = .67$), suggesting that testing alone does not account for the improved scores (Cook & Campbell, 1979). One way to rule out other reasons for these improved attitudes is to compare our parents' scores to those of similar parents who were not receiving any type of family support service (Cook & Campbell, 1979); however, we did not have access to a formal control or a no-service comparison group. Instead, we compared the programs with each other, using multiple regression analysis to adjust for any preservice differences among participants. This cross-program design allows for the assessment of the relative effectiveness of assorted interventions when control or no-treatment comparison groups are not available, as is often the case in evaluation research (Berkeley Planning Associates, 1977; Daro, 1988; Weiss, 1972), when programs have the same objective but provide different services, and when programs assess outcomes with the same measures (Weiss, 1972).

To strengthen this design, we designated the program operated by Congreso as the comparison program.[1] Two factors prompted this decision. First, Congreso's parent education program lasted for 10 weeks, the briefest intervention of the nine programs, which caused us to select it as the "minimal-service" comparison group. Second, this program served the largest number of parents, ensuring a conservative test of program impacts, as smaller-sized programs would need to produce substantial effects to overcome the difference in sample size. Although we cannot definitively attribute improvements by participants to program involvement, the comparative design provides some indication of program effectiveness and is particularly useful for examining whether programmatic differences in the type or frequency of services received by the parent correspond to improvements in parenting attitudes and practices.

In fact, this more careful scrutiny revealed that parents at only one program improved significantly more than parents receiving services at Congreso. Multiple regression analyses found that, after controlling for initial familial differences, parents participating in services offered by FSA of Bucks County ($T = -2.3, p < .02$) were the only group to significantly reduce their child abuse potential. To arrive at this finding, we first controlled for factors hypothesized to explain differing performance on the final CAP, such as initial CAP scores and parental characteristics (e.g., maternal age, education, marital status, source of referral, income level). Next, we examined the effect of program attendance and finally, service intensity which we defined as weekly program contacts, to discover if these service characteristics influenced parenting practices. For a more detailed discussion of the methodology, see Resource A. In the high-risk analyses discussed later, we also saw a strong, positive correlation between involvement with FSA of Bucks County and improved parental attitudes toward child rearing.

In attempting to understand why participation in services at FSA of Bucks County produced the most significant declines in punitive child-rearing attitudes, we noticed that two characteristics distinguished this particular program from the other projects. First, FSA of Bucks County served a much higher portion of married couples than did the other programs, probably because of its location in a suburban community, whereas the other programs were housed in inner-city neighborhoods with higher rates of single parenthood. Second, FSA of Bucks County primarily offered two services. Like several programs, parents could attend a weekly parent education group, the Family Life Education series, that focused on topics such as child development, discipline, money management, and self-esteem. In addition, this program was the only one to provide intensive counseling services for parents, with or without their children. After a comprehensive intake process, the parents met with a trained counselor on a regular basis to address problems identified through intake.

We think that the positive impact of this program may suggest that counseling services, a more traditional social work approach, warrant greater attention when designing family support programs, especially for use with two-parent families. Couples seeking prevention services may be involved in high levels of marital conflict or stress that, in turn, increase their potential to physically harm a child. Greater attention needs to be paid to the possibility that reducing relationship tension through counseling may substantially ameliorate negative parenting behaviors for couples. Transactional theories of parenting support this approach (Cicchetti & Lynch, 1993; Vondra & Belsky, 1993). According to the transactional model, caregiving is directly influenced by changes occurring in the immediate family environment such that increases in marital tension will lead to more aversive child rearing, whereas greater harmony will result in improved caregiving. Interventions that can successfully lower parental conflict will then foster caregiving, as seemed to be the case with parents attending FSA of Bucks County.

Another hypothesis deserving future research attention concerns the inclusion of husbands or fathers in these counseling services. Though we did not collect CAP scores on the fathers, greater maternal improvements may have been achieved at this program because both caregivers were more likely to attend services at FSA of Bucks County than at the other eight programs. We contend that maternal attitudes and behaviors are more likely to change if other family members are also exposed to intervention efforts. Indeed, ecological theory would suggest that working with as many family members as possible will help fashion a more nurturing child-rearing environment than focusing solely on the primary caregiver whose caregiving is influenced by the beliefs and actions of those around her. To date, however, few evaluations have looked at how fathers and other important caregivers respond to support services, though some argue that such research is critical for designing effective interventions (Guterman, 1997).

We also observed one other trend in these regressions with important guidance for the establishment of "critical" service elements in family support efforts (Guterman, 1997; McCurdy, 1996). The way a family finds out about a support program may influence program success. Regardless of their initial level of risk, parents who entered the Penn programs at the suggestion of a friend, neighbor, or on their own accord (e.g., informal source) improved more over time than those who were referred to services by professional sources, such as a social worker or doctor ($T = -2.5$, $p < .01$). One likely reason this occurs is because families who are inspired to seek out services on their own also possess greater motivation to improve caregiving. However, we think that another factor helps to explain this relationship. Though hard to measure, the perceived stigma attached to involvement in a parenting service is likely to be reduced if the family chooses to enter the program or if someone who resembles the parent recommends it. Indeed, a large portion of word-of-mouth referrals signals a successful program in the community's eyes. As noted in Chapter 2, programs engaged in aggressive, community-based outreach, such as door-to-door canvassing, achieved greater success in recruiting and retaining participants from informal sources than programs relying on outreach to professionals and community agencies. Parents recruited directly from the community also are more likely to remain in a prevention program, complete the full service component, and, as we saw in the foregoing discussion, gain more from these services. This combination of findings leads us to recommend that family support programs make these labor intensive, communitywide efforts to enroll parents, especially new programs attempting to establish a participant base.

We next looked at whether staff saw changes in parental attitudes over the course of services for the 681 parents (81%) with both entry and exit data. Given the drawbacks noted earlier with the staff assessment measure and our inability to use statistical methods to control for preservices differences among participants, less confidence should be placed in these program comparisons than in the preceding discussion of CAP scores. We did find, however, that the overall reduction in CAP scores corresponded to the staff's assessment that the typical parent substantially reduced her likelihood to engage in excessive corporal punishment. According to staff, 31% of these mothers became less likely to use corporal punishment, 10% were viewed as more likely, and 59% had not changed by the end of services. Staff made similar ratings of change regarding potential for emotional neglect. To a lesser degree, staff noted significant declines in the parents' potential to engage in inadequate supervision. For example, 25% of the parents were rated as less likely to provide inadequate supervision at the end of services, 62% stayed the same, and 13% increased their risk for this behavior by the time they left the program. Staff also assessed changes in the likelihood that parents would engage in three other forms of neglect (i.e., medical, educational, and physical) and fail to protect their child; however, so few parents were perceived as at risk for these behaviors that an examination of change was not feasible.

As with physical abuse potential, we observed that parents at some programs benefited more than those attending others. Group comparisons[2] (see Resource B) suggested that parents who attended prevention services at APM, Congreso, Crime Prevention, and FSA of Bucks County made the most significant progress in ameliorating their propensity to use excessive corporal punishment, to fail to provide adequate child supervision, and to emotionally neglect a child. In addition, the average parent who attended Philadelphia Society achieved notable reductions with corporal punishment and emotional neglect. We did not discern any underlying commonalities in program structure or participant background to explain the relative success of these five programs.

The High-Risk Participant

Answering our second research question, whether voluntary family support services benefited the most disadvantaged families, first entailed an examination of those parents with scores of 215 or more on CAP, a score that places the respondent in the high-risk category on this instrument (Milner, 1986). Though limiting our focus to the most vulnerable parents reduced much of the initial demographic differences among program participants, some remained. For example, APM and YSI served parents with lower incomes and educational attainment than the other programs. Parents at APM also had significantly higher initial CAP scores than the parents at the six other programs. In contrast, the participants at FSA of Bucks County continued to represent the most advantaged sample. We statistically adjusted for these differences before measuring program impact with CAP.

In line with the findings from other studies (see Berlin et al., 1998; MacMillan, MacMillan, Offord, Griffith, & MacMillan, 1994; Olds & Kitzman, 1993; Wekerle & Wolfe, 1993), the restricted analyses of high-risk families suggest that child abuse prevention services may be more effective with parents experiencing numerous challenges to adequate functioning. For the 217 parents (44%) who entered prevention services with high CAP scores (over 214), the typical parent significantly decreased her score by 50 points, a 16% reduction over initial scores ($p < .001$). In these analyses, we had to exclude participants from two programs, Alternatives and Family Service of Philadelphia, due to insufficient numbers of parents meeting the high-risk definition. Group t tests (see Figure 3.2) demonstrated a substantial decline in punitive attitudes among

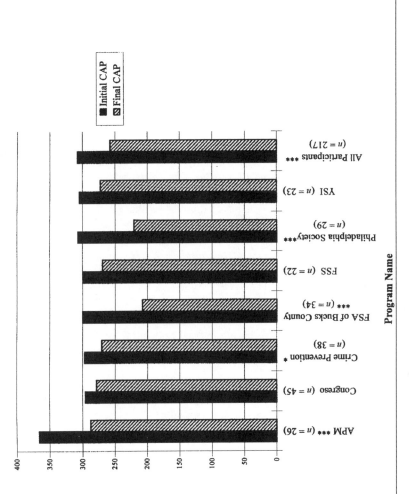

Figure 3.2. Change in CAP Scores for High-Risk[a] Participants

a. Participants scoring 215 or higher on the initial CAP (excludes Alternatives and FSP with $n < 10$).
$N = 217$; *$p < .05$; **$p < .01$; ***$p < .001$.

high-risk parents at the seven remaining programs ranging from 18 points at Congreso to 92 points at FSA of Bucks County.

Because we selected parents based on their high CAP scores, we had to guard against regression to the mean as the primary explanation for these large declines in scores (Cook & Campbell, 1979). In this case, regression could occur because parents with initially high scores will "regress" toward the average score over time. As the average initial score for all participants is 219 as compared to 308 ($SD = 58$) for the high-risk parents, a natural regression to the group mean can masquerade as an actual program effect.

To help rule out this explanation, we again employed the same multiple regression model as before with Congreso as the limited service, comparison program (see Resource B for regression results). The regressions first indicated that parents who entered the program with a relatively high child abuse potential still look worse at the end of services than those who came into services with initially lower CAP scores. Although demographic factors do not substantially explain final CAP scores in these regressions, never-married mothers had significantly higher CAP scores ($T = 2.5$, $p < .02$) at the end of services as compared to ever-married mothers. In addition, younger parents and those referred by an informal source posted somewhat lower scores on their final CAP ($p < .10$). After controlling for initial CAP scores and entry characteristics, 16% of the variance in final CAP scores was explained ($p < .001$). When we added attendance at the seven programs, this amount increased by 7% ($p < .01$). Of the seven programs, participation at two correlated with substantially lower CAP scores. Attending services at FSA of Bucks County ($T = -2.5$, $p < .01$) and at Philadelphia Society for Services to Children ($T = -2.4$, $p < .02$) corresponded to lower final CAP scores for high-risk parents.

The use of quasi-experimental methods, a common strategy in program evaluation, means that the observed changes in parenting practices cannot be definitely attributed to enrollment at FSA of Bucks County or Philadelphia Society for Services to Children (Cook & Campbell, 1979). However, the pattern of results indicates that we can discount regression to the mean as a cause for change in physical child abuse potential (i.e., CAP scores) where participation at FSA of Bucks County predicted lower CAP scores. In both the overall and high-risk analyses, parents at Bucks County did not have the highest CAP scores, yet they showed the most improvement. It seems unlikely that statistical regression (Cook & Campbell, 1979) was producing this effect, as we would then expect to see the greatest gains among programs serving parents with the highest CAP scores.

The results first suggested that even when limited to high-risk families, the counseling and Family Life Education courses offered by FSA of Bucks County promoted improved parental attitudes over time. Again, we were led to posit that this service combination prompted two-parent families to change their views on the appropriate use of physical punishment. Next, we sought to understand why parents involved with Philadelphia Society appeared to outperform those attending other services. In this instance, the combination of home visits and parent support groups provided by Philadelphia Society produced parenting improvements with its relatively large high-risk teen population. This finding may suggest that home visitation and peer support groups help increase both the number and types of social supports available to the teen who is often more isolated than the typical parent due to the "off-time" nature of her child's birth (Hagestad & Neugarten, 1985). Indeed, supportive services for the teen might be especially important if the child's birth has caused or exacerbated conflict between the teen and her mother. We hypothesized that advice and encouragement of the teen's parenting skills from peers as well as a home visitor could provide the impetus needed to refrain from potentially harmful parenting practices, for two reasons. First, as teens typically seek autonomy from their parents during adolescence (Liebert & Wicks-Nelson, 1981), they may be more willing to listen to peers and nonrelatives about child care practices and to benefit from these diverse perspectives. Second, the support group format may be particularly effective with teens due to the importance of peers in adolescence. Because adolescent mothers can encounter conflict with their families and isolation from their friends due to their premature parental role, we believe that the additional supports offered by the home visitor in concert with the peer support group help reduce conflict and isolation, thereby enhancing the teen's parenting abilities.

When we turned our attention to the parents perceived by staff to be at highest risk, we also saw improvements in parenting attitudes. All 268 parents initially rated by staff as at least somewhat likely to engage in excessive physical punishment, emotional neglect, or inadequate supervision were included in these analyses. By the end of services, close to half (43%) were no longer viewed as likely to harm a child. Staff rated one quarter of these parents as likely to engage in one form of maltreatment, down from 39%. The number believed to be at risk for all three behaviors was cut in half, from 31% to 15%.

Group t tests indicate that the average high-risk parent at every program experienced a significant reduction in all three maltreating behaviors; however, the program comparisons revealed that some programs had greater impacts on their highest-risk families than others (see Resource B). We found that parents at Congreso and APM were the most likely to improve in the area of corporal punishment; those at ending Congreso also reduced their risk for inadequate supervision more than their high-risk counterparts at the other programs. The Kruskal-Wallis (Downing & Clark, 1997) analysis of mean rank suggests that high-risk parents at Congreso and FSA of Bucks County achieved the most success in reducing their potential for emotional neglect. High-risk parents at the remaining programs do not differ markedly.

The fact that parents at Congreso did not demonstrate similar improvements on CAP as on the staff's assessment of corporal punishment raises questions, as both measures should tap into the same construct: physical abuse potential. Problems with the administration of the staff assessment measure at Congreso reduced the comparability of these data to those collected at the other programs. In many cases, the participants completed the staff assessment form rather than Congreso program staff. Still, the fact that the participants themselves believed that they had reduced their risk by attending the Congreso workshops is of note. This belief suggests that these parents have increased their feelings of self-efficacy regarding their child-rearing practices. It is hoped that increased self-efficacy will eventually lead to higher levels of self-esteem, reduced stress in the parent-child relationship, and more confidence to try alternative discipline strategies.

As we could not statistically control for initial participant differences when looking at staff ratings of maltreatment potential, it is unclear whether these changes reflected substantial movement on the part of parents or whether any program proved most effective. What may be more important is that staff noted fewer gains with respect to inadequate supervision, suggesting an area for future exploration. On the one hand, parents might find it easier to accept and apply alternative discipline strategies than to pay closer attention to their child's daily activities and whereabouts, especially if the parent is preoccupied with her or his own needs. Neglectful behaviors often appear more entrenched and less amenable to change through family support efforts than more aggressive parental practices, such as yelling or hitting (Polansky, Gaudin, & Kilpatrick, 1992). On the other hand, these findings could reflect the attention providers pay to discipline issues as opposed to neglect. In fact, our on-site visits suggested that most Penn programs did indeed emphasize restraint from physical forms of discipline. Providers typically devoted considerable amounts of service time to discussions, role-plays, and modeling around discipline. This topic also frequently arose in parent support group discussions. In contrast, we observed fewer sessions considering how to appropriately supervise a child, although child safety issues were reviewed.

Staff viewed emotional neglect as the biggest child-rearing hurdle facing these high-risk parents, with 66% initially rated as likely to engage in this form of maltreatment. Emotional neglect has long been viewed as one of the most harmful forms of maltreatment (Garbarino, 1980). Estimates of its frequency, however, indicate that mandated reporters have observed substantially fewer cases of emotional neglect than physical abuse, physical neglect, and sexual abuse (U.S. Department of Health & Human Services, 1998; Wang & Daro, 1998). In contrast, a recent national incidence study reports a large increase in the number of emotionally neglected children nationwide (Sedlak & Broadhurst, 1996).

Although we do not know if the higher prevalence found in the current study occurred because the Penn providers had greater knowledge of the family than do mandated reporters or because the incidence of emotional neglect is much higher in Philadelphia, the need to prevent emotional neglect emerged as a primary concern for program providers, even though few planners had specifically listed this intent as a program goal.

Program Impacts on Ethnically Similar Populations

Traditional research designs tend to rely on cross-race comparisons that mask potential differences within racial groups regarding parenting practices (Sheldon & Parker, 1992). For example, prevention evaluations typically look at whether a given service—say, home visiting—is more effective with white versus Hispanic families. Rarely do such studies address more informative questions, such as whether African American families are more likely to benefit from a parent-child play group as opposed to a home-visiting service. In this study, we were fortunate to have a racially diverse sample that allowed us to explore this question. Initially, we had hoped to compare the programs serving Hispanic communities as well as those serving African American neighborhoods. The parents attending the two Hispanic programs, however, bore so little resemblance to each other in terms of age, marital status, number of children, and initial CAP scores that we could not statistically make these comparisons.

Instead, we focused on the five programs located in urban, African American neighborhoods: Crime Prevention ($n = 87$), FSP ($n = 25$), FSS ($n = 74$), Philadelphia Society ($n = 59$), and YSI ($n = 111$). As a group, the five programs served predominately low-income families, with over 80% receiving some type of public assistance. Most parents had three children and were not married at the time they enrolled in services. In addition, the parents at the five programs did not differ significantly on their initial CAP scores. There were some differences, however, as Crime Prevention, FSP, and FSS typically served older parents (age 26 or older) who had received a high school degree. In contrast, Philadelphia Society and YSI worked with a younger set of parents (age 21 or younger), the majority of whom had never finished high school.

In terms of service distinctions, Crime Prevention, FSS, and YSI provided the most comprehensive packages by offering a combination of home visits, parent education groups, parent support groups, limited counseling, and parent-child play groups. Parents attending FSP had a choice of parent education or parent support groups, whereas those involved with Philadelphia Society could receive home visits, attend the parent support groups, or both. Furthermore, the length of time a parent could attend any of these programs varied greatly, with those at YSI participating for close to a year as compared to only 10 weeks for parents at FSP.

Although parents at Philadelphia Society posted the largest reduction in CAP scores over time, our multiple regression analyses revealed that the programs serving African American neighborhoods produced similar effects on child abuse potential once we statistically accounted for initial differences in participant risk and demographic backgrounds (see Resource B). However, the staff's assessment of parental likelihood for maltreatment revealed two interesting outcomes. First, we found that participants at FSP were viewed as substantially less likely to reduce their potential for excessive corporal punishment than parents who received services at the other programs. In fact, staff rated parents at FSP as the least likely to change on any maltreating behavior. In this instance, the major service distinction between FSP and the other four programs is service duration, with parents at FSP enrolled for only 10 weeks as compared to a minimum of 16 weeks at the other programs. Other studies (see Gomby, Larson, Lewit, & Behrman, 1993) also reveal that brief interventions have resulted in fewer child-rearing benefits for African American parents.

The other finding of note involved parents at Crime Prevention, who made the greatest strides in lowering their potential for emotional neglect, though this relationship may not remain if one were to control for initial differences among the parents. Despite this limitation, the greater progress by Crime Prevention parents suggests some interesting hypotheses. As Crime Prevention staff served the oldest participants, this may indicate that problems with emotional neglect can be more readily addressed with an older and more highly educated group of participants. In terms of programmatic differences that may account for this finding, Crime Prevention's provision of a substantial number of parent-child play group sessions may enable providers to directly work with African American mothers on this aspect of parenting. The opportunity to observe and intervene in parent-child interactions may be necessary to significantly reduce a mother's tendency to emotionally neglect her child. FSS was the only other program among this group where participants engaged in a substantial number of parent-child play group sessions. The fact that these parents posted the second greatest gains with emotional neglect lends some validity to the second hypothesis.

LESSONS LEARNED

Although the study's methodological limitations restricted our ability to make causal inferences about program effects, the array of findings has led us to believe that interventions succeed when the service offered closely matches the perceived needs of the family. Stated another way, one service design, no matter how well-conceived and implemented, will not achieve success with all or even most vulnerable families (McCurdy, 1996; Weiss, 1993). The diversity among parents seeking out these support programs, in terms of risk for child-rearing problems, access to other support sources, and reason for attending services in the first place, all influence the type of service most likely to attract, engage, and retain the family in the program. Appropriately matching a given service with family characteristics; using recruitment strategies that maximize informal referral sources; and offering frequent, lengthy, and accessible services all potentially contribute to a successful family support program. Furthermore, we found evidence that voluntary prevention services can produce positive impacts with some of the highest-risk families, suggesting that prevention efforts may find a market even in extremely disadvantaged communities. Last, our findings suggest that cultural issues need greater attention by all those involved with the design and implementation of support services (Daro & McCurdy, 1994; Slaughter-Defoe, 1993). The exploratory look at programs serving African American neighborhoods suggested some differential program impacts for emotionally neglectful families. Future research should probe such relationships to explicitly assess this issue of cultural compatibility between the service and family.

Although this chapter has generated more hypotheses than answers for designing effective services, we offer the following lessons learned to help guide program development:

Service Providers

- Planners and providers need to determine what types of families are most likely to benefit from the planned service. Our findings suggest that the following combinations appeared to promote less punitive child-rearing attitudes: adolescent, single mothers receiving both parent support groups and home visits and two-parent families attending counseling services.

- Interventions that allow for direct modeling of nurturing parenting practices, such as parent-child play groups, may be most productive for parents at risk for emotional neglect. Such groups can provide a safe and nonthreatening environment to observe and try out new parenting skills.

- Given the prominence of neglect in the United States and the high potential for inadequate supervision and emotional estrangement from the child found in these Philadelphia families, methods for enhancing parental involvement and supervision should be a major focus of any curriculum or service directed at child rearing.

- We recommend that programs include, whenever possible, in-home services, transportation assistance, and child care services to help families maintain long-term involvement in family support programs.

Funders and Policymakers

- To date, the bulk of programmatic and research dollars have addressed the prevention of physical or sexual abuse. Although some recent initiatives at the federal level have examined neglect, other major program funders have not been as generous in this area. We recommend that significantly more resources be directed toward the prevention and treatment of neglect.

● Funders often choose between funding a service designed to serve many people or one that assists fewer parents but in a more comprehensive fashion. We argue that emphasizing quality over quantity is a cost-effective approach in the long run and should guide grant-making decisions.

● Instead of emphasizing one particular service type to apply universally, as did the U.S. Advisory Board on Child Abuse and Neglect in 1991 (Krugman, 1993), we believe that diverse families most likely need a range of service options. We advocate that a universal process to assess parental needs be the first step in establishing a nationwide family support system.

Researchers

● Although the timing of service initiation has garnered recent attention (Gomby et al., 1993; Guterman, 1997), the service initiation *process* may be just as important. Future research efforts should examine the link between program effectiveness and recruitment method and help identify recruitment strategies that enhance word of mouth and self-referrals among vulnerable and at-risk populations.

● This study and others would benefit from a stronger methodological design that included more outcome measures, a no-treatment comparison or control group, and outside data collectors. Finding sufficient funds to support more rigorous studies is often problematic but necessary to advance the field of family support.

● As noted earlier, few studies have investigated ways to prevent neglectful caretaking. Given its prevalence and detrimental impacts, social scientists need to focus on this problem to generate findings that can assist programs in working with neglectful parents.

NOTES

1. To ensure that this decision did not bias the results, we ran the same regressions using different programs as the comparison group and still achieved the same outcomes, suggesting that the programmatic findings are robust.

2. In these analyses, we first used group *t* tests to assess what sites experienced a significant change between program entry and exit. We then employed the Kruskal-Wallis (Downing & Clark, 1997) one-way analysis of variance to determine how the programs ranked among each other.

CHAPTER 4

Long-Term Changes
in Parenting Practices

Rarely do program evaluators have the opportunity to assess participants beyond the program's end. Only a handful of the many evaluations of child abuse prevention programs we reviewed examined participants' progress after service termination (Barth, 1991; Olds et al., 1986; Olds et al., 1997; Wesch & Lutzker, 1991). Overall, these studies yielded mixed results about the long-term effectiveness of programs to increase child safety and alter parenting practices.

These studies suggested that family support interventions have sustained influence for some types of participants and not others. Specifically, economically disadvantaged, white, first-time parents gained the most from various types of early support and intervention. For instance, some of those who had received 2 years of nurse home visitation when they were adolescents were more likely to be enrolled in school and to have had fewer subsequent pregnancies 4 years after initiation of services than their counterparts (Olds et al., 1986). These same women 15 years later were less likely to have been perpetrators of child abuse maltreatment and had fewer subsequent children, months on AFDC, behavioral impairments from drug or alcohol abuse, convictions, and number of days jailed over the 15-year interval than the control group (Olds et al., 1997). Similarly, poor first-time parents who engaged in a comprehensive parenting program, including the provision of day care, showed gains in the areas of mother's education, family economic independence, and the child's school performance (Seitz, Rosenbaum, & Apfel, 1985).

In this chapter, we explore the influence of the Penn prevention programs on parenting practices and attitudes 2 years after the program's end. The degree to which the prevention programs altered parenting practices beyond the life of the program provided another way of measuring success. The follow-up data, collected through in-depth interviews with 69 former participants 2 years after program termination, showed that 75% of the parents continued to apply what they had learned from the programs. Such gains were most prominent for parents who started the programs at the higher end of the risk continuum. With regard to specific parenting practices 2 years after the program's end, the average parent continued to exhibit decreased potential for physical abuse (measured by the CAP), a decline in the use of corporal punishment, an increased use of alternative discipline techniques, greater emotional involvement with children, and an increased awareness of the detrimental impacts of hitting, yelling, and swearing on their children's emotional well-being. In addition, parents remarked on some noteworthy changes in parent-child interaction as evidenced by the changes in activities with their children.

It is also important to understand what, if any, of the service characteristics influenced long-term change. We examine the participants' retrospective views of what services were the most important. High-risk parents consistently named three specific program aspects that remained noteworthy to them, even 2 years later: group discussions, activities with parent-child interaction time, and staff relations. We use participants' quotes to indicate how such program factors assisted these particular parents.

Long-term outcomes include parental self-report of frequency of discipline practices, parental description of child behaviors that led to punishment, and parental accounts of the most recent disciplinary action and the circumstances surrounding it. In addition, parents were asked to respond to a number of typical, age-specific child-rearing scenarios. Last, CAP, the standardized self-report measure used to assess immediate program impacts, was readministered at the 2-year follow-up point, providing a consistent measure to assess attitudinal change over time.

Our follow-up study differed from previous follow-up studies in three important ways. We assessed postprogram child abuse potential and discipline practices rather than focusing on child abuse reports. Although we believe that such a variety of indicators enhances the validity and reliability of the follow-up findings, our choice of measures differs so vastly from previous evaluation that it makes linking our findings with those of other studies impossible. Second, we attempt to link long-term outcomes with specific program characteristics, such as program length and frequency and type of service offered. Last, as previous follow-up studies of child abuse prevention interventions primarily examined home-visiting programs, we know very little about the lasting influences of group-based child abuse prevention activities. Our findings help extend the limited knowledge base regarding the relative importance of program and staff characteristics on retention of program gains, the types of parental attitude or behavior changes most likely to endure, the process parents undergo as they attempt to alter their behavior or attitudes, and the extent to which retention of program gains differs, depending on family.

THE FOLLOW-UP SAMPLE

We drew the follow-up sample from the 192 participants who had completed services during the initial round of funding, during the years 1989 to 1992. Initially, we had intended to select 10 participants from each of the nine prevention programs from this pool. As we knew selecting from each program would ensure a heterogeneous sample, the only criteria for selection into the follow-up sample included having both a baseline and termination CAP. Due to staff changes and the loss of the master list at one of the programs, we were unable to obtain as many follow-up sample members as we had originally planned. We interviewed a small number of the 1989-1992 participant impact sample members ($n = 69$), hereafter referred to as the follow-up sample.

The generalizability of the responses from this follow-up group to the larger participant sample depended on the comparability of the two samples. As shown in Table 4.1, members of the follow-up sample, on average, had initiated the programs with fewer economic resources, larger families, greater numbers of parenting problems, and higher child abuse potential than their counterparts in the full sample. In essence, the follow-up sample represented participants who entered the programs with the greatest number of parenting challenges.

As an analytical approach, in lieu of a comparison group, we found it useful to assess the long-term program impacts by comparing those who initiated services as low risk according to their beginning CAP score with those who scored as high risk at program entry. Viewing the follow-up sample in this manner, 50% ($n = 35$) were low risk, with an average initial CAP score of 139; 49% ($n = 34$) of the sample scored in the higher-risk group, with an average score of 304. Even though the follow-up sample is split evenly between those who began the programs as low risk versus high risk, we shall see throughout this chapter that the high-risk follow-up participants represented a unique group of the most disadvantaged families who engaged in the Penn programs.

Discipline Practices

All of the programs addressed the use of alternative discipline strategies, such as time out, denial of privileges, and restriction. The evidence presented in the previous chapter clearly suggests that at the program's end, the average parent achieved significant strides in this area. Two years later, one third of the

TABLE 4.1 Comparison of the Follow-up Sample With the Full Participant Sample
(by percentage)

	Original Participant Sample[a] (n = 291)	Follow-up Sample (n = 69)
Mother's age		
19 or less	16.4	19.1
20 to 24 years	17.1	20.5
25 to 29 years	24.7	17.8
30 plus years	40.5	43.8
Race		
African American	35.0	60.2
Hispanic	20.6	32.8
White	44.3	19.1
Marital status		
Currently married	29.1	26.0
Previously married	15.4	17.8
Never married	30.5	39.7
Living together	9.6	20.5
Number of children		
One	40.2	29.3
Two	23.3	34.2
Three	20.6	20.5
Four or more	14.7	20.5
Household income		
Less than $15,000	36.4	58.9
$15,000 to $24,999	14.0	6.8
$25,000 plus	25.7	13.6

a. The original participant sample consisted of parents involved in the first round of data collection between 1989 and 1992 (i.e., Cohort 1). All comparisons are nonsignificant.

follow-up sample continued to improve their discipline practices, whereas one third did not. The remaining parents used the same discipline techniques they employed at program termination.

CAP Scores After Program Termination

As shown in Figure 4.1, participants' CAP scores remained fairly stable after they left the program. High-risk parents evidenced the greatest decline during services, yet one third retained an elevated potential for child maltreatment at the time we conducted our follow-up interviews. The following section describes the ways in which some parents overcame their aggressive parenting habits, whereas others found it difficult or unnecessary to change their ways. What should be of particular interest to service providers is the type of behavior that triggered a hostile reaction from the more aggressive mothers. When such mothers felt that a child had talked back to them or acted in an "out of control" manner, tempers rose and physical punishment ensued.

The sustained improvement occurred among those who were high risk at program entry. Of the initially high-risk participants, 40% were no longer high risk at the follow-up point; however, another one third did remain at risk for child maltreatment according to their CAP scores.

Current Discipline Practices

The continuing decline in CAP scores was echoed in parental comments about current child-rearing practices. When asked about discipline usage and normal responses to "typical" child behaviors, however, we begin to see that changing parental behavior is not a straightforward endeavor.

Multiple Forms of Discipline

The responses to the question about discipline used the last time each of their children acted out indicated that parents who spank and yell rely on multiple forms of discipline more often than those who never engage in these methods. The data presented in Table 4.2 illustrate the way parents disciplined in response to a real situation with their children as named by the parents. This approach yielded a more complex discipline pattern than the drop in CAP scores might lead one to believe. Looking across the categories depicting the frequency of spanking shows that those who spank monthly (40% of the entire sample) or spank 11 times a year or less (30%) employed numerous discipline strategies as contrasted with those who never spank (30%), who named only three methods of discipline. Specifically, participants who never spanked relied exclusively on time out, restriction, or talking through the problem with the child.

A former participant, the mother of four children, is representative of those who yell or spank frequently. She reported using three different types of discipline in response to the fact that her 7-year-old daughter had two Fs on her report card. This mother, who spanked and yelled at her two youngest children monthly,

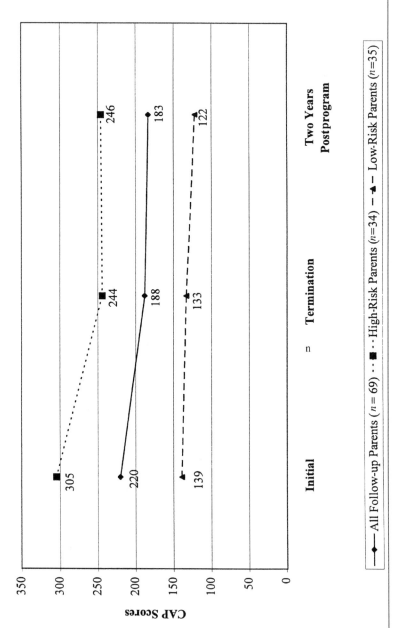

Figure 4.1. Change in CAP Scores for Follow-up Parents

TABLE 4.2 Most Recent Parental Discipline Practice by Frequency of Spanking (by percentage)

Never Spanks (n = 27)	*Spanks Less Than Monthly* (n = 20)	*Spanks Monthly* (n = 20)
Deny privileges (29)	Deny privileges (14)	Ignore action (13)
Discuss action (29)	Deny privileges, hit, and yell (14)	Discuss action and hit (13)
Ignore action (14)	Time out (10)	Hit and time out (13)
Discuss and time out (14)	Hit and discuss or deny privileges (9.6)	Hit and discuss or deny privileges (8.6)
Deny privileges and discuss action (14)		

mentioned hitting, denying privileges, and restriction in response to her child's report card. Furthermore, although she acknowledged the benefits of alternative forms of punishment, saying that "taking away TV privileges is more painful" for her daughter than hitting or screaming, she continued to resort to hitting.

Among those who spanked frequently, the form of discipline employed often showed minimal relation to the severity of the child's behavior. The types of behavior that elicited the physical discipline reactions included whining, fighting with siblings, challenging the parent, desiring attention, and school-related matters. For example, "demanding attention" proved to be one of the more prevalent behaviors that prompted a discipline response from at least one fifth of the parents. Punishment for this behavior ranged from spanking to yelling to ignoring the child.

One of the factors complicating this analysis was that parents had children of all ages. It is interesting that this configuration of behaviors and corresponding discipline practices persisted even for parents with children up to age 13. Parents generally refrained from hitting their older children because they reported that they feared retaliation from their children. Nonetheless, the multiple discipline usage pattern held across age groups.

Response to Specific Behaviors

During the course of the interviews, parents discussed why and in what instances they hit their children. A clear trend emerged between the subsample of those who hit frequently and those who did not. Parents who hit frequently did so to assert their authority as well as to "maintain control" of their children. Talking back to their parents and throwing a tantrum in public also proved to be behaviors that prompted a physical response from the parents who resorted to unhealthy discipline regularly. In contrast, those who hit infrequently did so judiciously, generally when children were perceived to be in danger. The following quote illustrates this last point. A mother from Philadelphia Society describes how she decides to discipline. Referring to her 2-year-old and 4-year-old, she says,

> If they play with plugs or matches or anything like that, I'll smack them. But if they do something like play in my lipstick in my pocketbook, something a child would do and it's not dangerous, I'll make them stand in the corner for something like that.

Other former participants who rarely used physical discipline echoed the fact that they only spanked when the child did something dangerous.

The question, "How did you handle the last time one of your children talked back to you?" produced the most pronounced difference between parents who spanked monthly and those who never spanked, relative to other questions and scenarios. Among those who spanked regularly, the most frequent response was to hit the child, as cited by 36% of the parents. A mother of three children, aged 4, 2, and 1, talked about the disrespectful incident involving her 4-year-old in this way:

> He was playing with the water although he got a cold and he like to throw water on the kids. So I told him not to play with the water and I went to smack his hand and he says "Don't smack my hand . . . you ain't my mom, who do you think you is?" I calmly got the belt and showed him who I was. I said, "I'm your mother. You don't talk to me like that."

This mother is representative of those who were clearly trying to establish themselves as the parent to their pre-school-age children. It is also important to point out that many of the parents using hitting to establish their authority were adolescents at the birth of their first child. It is plausible that these moms were maturing into their role as mother as they got older. However, because parental boundaries were not clearly established between the mother and the child earlier in the child's development, the child may have already developed a pattern of challenging the mother's authority.

In contrast, former participants who never spanked stuck to this policy even when their children talked back to them. These parents responded that they would talk with their child about the reasons they should not be disrespectful. A mother who never yells or hits, from the YSI program, responded in this manner, telling her 5-year-old son,

> Respect is due to all adults, and you are a child and you do not talk back to me. You do not. When I tell you to do something, you get up and do it. I don't want to hear "I don't want to get it, I'm tired, this and that." Only way mommy won't ask you to do anything is if you are sick. But you do not talk back to me or any adults. We are all adults: your nana, your daddy, your aunt, your uncle, your teachers.

The scenario depicting a toddler-aged child throwing a tantrum in the grocery store over something the mother would not buy for him produced a range of discipline responses. Those named most often included ignoring or walking away (21%), hitting or spanking (14%), talking to the child (12.5%), buying whatever the child was throwing a tantrum to have (11%), and removing the child from the store (10%). Among parents who spanked monthly, the most frequent response was to ignore or walk away from the child, followed by purchasing the item the child desired, and hitting the child. Removing the child from the store proved to be the strategy most frequently exercised by the parents least likely to spank, followed by talking to the child or ignoring the child. In their responses to the tantrum scenario, parents raised additional factors that influenced their reactions. Some of the mothers mentioned feeling bad about not being able to afford what their children wanted, though they often gave in and purchased the item anyway, or they tried to talk the child into wanting something less expensive.

The other issue raised consistently by parents about this scenario was what others in the store might think of them. In other parts of the interview, parents, especially those who spanked frequently, appeared overly concerned about what others thought of them, giving the impression that they felt others would judge their parenting based on how unruly their children were. It should also be pointed out that some parents knew not to hit their children in public. For most of these mothers, however, a child talking back appears to pose a greater threat to parental control than temper tantrums.

Discipline Practices From a National Perspective

In addition to CAP, which provides the only consistent indicator of participant progress over time, participants responded to survey questions designed to assess current parental discipline practices. These same questions have been used for the past 9 years to determine parenting practices of a random sample of U.S. parents (Daro, 1998). As such, they allowed a comparison of the Penn participants' behavior and attitudes with the average U.S. parent.

We asked participants to report how often during the past 12 months they had used four specific types of discipline: (a) denying privileges, (b) confining to a

room, (c) insulting, and (d) spanking. Table 4.3 demonstrates that the Penn follow-up sample participants employed all discipline strategies to a greater degree
and with greater frequency than a random sample of U.S. parents. Fully two
thirds of the follow-up sample reported insulting their children, contrasted with
only 44% of the national sample; 82% spanked, compared with 52% of the national sample. On the other hand, the percentage of parents denying privileges in
both the national sample and the follow-up sample is strikingly similar. Ranking
the four techniques by parental usage revealed that denying privileges was
the most frequently used discipline strategy by parents in both samples, followed by confinement of a child to his or her room, then spanking, and finally,
yelling. Viewed in this manner, the follow-up sample's relative reliance on certain discipline patterns reflected those of the national sample, although with
greater magnitude.

The follow-up-sample parents disciplined their children more frequently
than their national counterparts. On average, compared with the national sample, they were 2 times as likely to deny privileges, 4 times more likely to confine
their children to their rooms, 5 times more likely to insult their children, and almost 6 times more likely to spank their children on a monthly basis. In contrast,
the national-sample parents tended to apply each of these methods fewer than 6
times per year. It is important to point out, however, that a certain percentage of
parents in both the Penn follow-up sample and the national sample refrained
completely from spanking or insulting their children. Of the Penn sample, 20%
never spanked their children, compared to 40% of the parents in the national
sample who never did so; 40% of the follow-up parents never insulted their children, contrasted with 54% of the national sample. That these differences are not
as striking as those related to monthly usage suggests that the follow-up sample
at 2 years postprogram is composed of parents at two ends of the discipline spectrum, those who spank and yell at their children continually and those who refrain entirely from these behaviors.

Although this analysis led us to believe that the Penn follow-up sample participants were using alternative forms of discipline, we were intrigued by the
frequency of discipline usage. On closer examination, we discovered that Penn
participants were using multiple forms of discipline. Rather than substituting
more positive forms of discipline for spanking and yelling at their children, the
follow-up sample appeared to be using these newly acquired discipline approaches in conjunction with spanking and yelling.

The survey questions also allowed the study team to assess parental attitudes
regarding the cumulative harm of selected discipline practices. Compared to the
national sample, the former Penn participants were more cognizant of the negative long-term impact of physical discipline. Nearly half of the Penn follow-up
sample readily perceived the detrimental impact of physical punishment on the

TABLE 4.3 Percentage of Follow-up Parents Using Specific Discipline Practices Compared With a National Parent Sample

Discipline Practice	2-Year Postprogram (n = 67)	National Sample, 1991 (n = 480)	National Sample, 1992 (n = 445)
Deny privileges			
Used in past year	80	76	83
Used in past month	33	16	8
Confine child to room			
Used in past year	82	57	53
Used in past month	39	9	3
Insult child			
Used in past year	66	44	4
Used in past month	32	6	2
Spank child			
Used in past year	82	52	53
Used in past month	40	7	2

NOTE: National estimates from Daro and Gelles (1992).

children's long-term emotional well-being. An additional one third of the parents reported that such punishment leads to long-term damage "occasionally" rather than "very often." The remaining 13% of the parents discerned little or no correlation between the two. These findings suggest that the programs increased the former participants' understanding of the detrimental impact of physical discipline beyond that of the average U.S. parent.

Nonetheless, as shown by the parents' willingness to spank and yell, a significant proportion did not translate their beliefs into action. Comparing the Penn follow-up sample's attitudes with the way they disciplined their children showed the incongruity between beliefs and actions. Surprisingly little correlation existed between the two. The one third of the follow-up-sample parents who spanked their children monthly viewed this behavior as detrimental. Even less consistency existed between believing yelling was harmful and practice, as 68% of former participants exercised this strategy on a monthly basis even though they acknowledged it as harmful. The following response from a former FSS participant shows her concern about the fact that she still yells and uses physical discipline on a monthly basis even though she is aware of the long-term detrimental impact on her children.

> *Interviewer:* Is there anything you would like to change about your parenting?
>
> *Respondent:* Yes. The hollering, the shoving.
>
> *Interviewer:* What do you wish you could be doing instead or how would you do it?
>
> *Respondent:* Talk. Talk more instead of hollering more. Every time I hear a commercial, it goes to my head, what children see they learn. They follow after their parents.

Other evaluations of prevention programs found similar incongruities between attitudes and practice (Wolfe, 1991). A precursor to changing behavior is to alter attitudes related to these behaviors. In this arena, the Penn programs made significant long-term inroads. It may be unrealistic to expect large degrees of continued improvement when parents are attempting to change such long-standing behavior, without continued support from some type of parenting program. Of those who maintained the practice of physical discipline, 30% articulated that they still wanted to change this behavior.

As we will see in the following chapter, another theme emerged while we were trying to understand the inconsistencies among parental responses to the discipline questions. All of the parents who spanked or yelled monthly reported that they had improved their parenting. Reviewing their responses showed that parents defined their own measures of success relative to their reference group, whether that be the parenting style used by their own parents or their childhood experience. For prevention programs serving high-risk mothers, to gauge program success, they should include assessments of these incremental changes. Allowing parents to describe success from their own frames of reference is often overlooked as a method for capturing these impacts.

The fact that parents from both the Penn sample and the national sample were more likely to spank their children than to yell at them deserves more attention. Both groups tended to view insulting a child as far more detrimental than spanking a child. A credible explanation is that parents may be responding to this question based on their own childhood experience. Although 60% of the Penn sample felt they were hit too hard as children, about 20% believed that they deserved it. In contrast, of the 82% reporting that they were yelled at too much, none of them felt they deserved it. Another likely explanation for the fact that yelling is perceived as more harmful than spanking could be the success of public awareness campaigns regarding verbal abuse. To the extent that the prevention programs stress this issue, they may reinforce participants' understanding about verbal abuse.

PARENT-CHILD ACTIVITIES

In addition to discipline strategies, all programs addressed parent-child interaction to some degree. Of the follow-up sample, 70% claimed that they altered the types of activities they did with their children as a direct result of prevention program involvement. These newly acquired activities included more outings (41%), spending more time with the child (29%), engaging in more educational activities (12%), or some combination of these three. Although high-risk and low-risk parents were equally likely to report that they had increased their interaction with their children, the specific way in which this was carried out differed by initial risk status. In particular, the high-risk parents were more likely to mention increased outings and increased educational activities.

Increased Outings

According to former participants, the programs had the greatest long-term impact on the parents' willingness to take their children on outings, such as to the Please Touch Children's Museum. Nearly half of the high-risk participants mentioned this change, as compared to one third of the low-risk participants. Prior to program participation, remarkably few of the high-risk parents took their children on educational or recreational outings. In fact, from their responses, most of them stayed at home all the time or occasionally left home to visit family.

Former participants talked about what had kept them from doing activities outside the home. An initially high-risk mother from Philadelphia Society remarked that her fear of violence kept her and her three small children, aged 4, 3, and 2 years, from doing more outside their home. But after participation in the program, she explained,

> Well, yeah. I could say that because I moved in the projects down here in South Philly, and I hate them. I'm terrified to death for bringing the kids out of the house. I am. I'm terrified of gun fire and stuff. But I started doing more things with them because I felt guilty about keeping them in inside. I don't allow them to play outside at all. I'll take them to McDonald's or I'll take them to the park and then here and in my son's school they send you home flyers and let you know what's going on in the neighborhood. I try to do more like this.

Another mother from Philadelphia Society explained how she had been responsible for her ailing mother, which prohibited her from taking her children out of the house. By obtaining her own house with the help of Philadelphia Society staff, this high-risk mother, who continued to improve after the program ended, became able to do more with her children. She revealed,

> Yeah. I was the type of person who stayed in the house a lot with them because I had a sick mother. Like I had no choice but to stay in with her and the kids. But now since I've got my own place, I take them out and stuff like that, plus they go to day care, and my son is in school and my daughter is in day care.

Undoubtedly, the stay-at-home behavior created frustration for both the children and the mother. With such limited outlets for children to expend their energy, it is understandable why parents might view their children as unruly—and therefore, to want "more control" over their children.

It is interesting that program staff never explicitly articulated increasing the parents' ability to take their children on outings as a goal of the programs, although improving parent-child interaction was a common goal. The majority of the sites took parents and children on field trips about twice a year. Yet from the participants' point of view, "getting out with their children" proved to be one of the most meaningful benefits they derived from the prevention programs. In part, this unintended consequence may be the result of attending center-based services, where field trips were an integral part of the program. Plausibly, once parents realized they could manage an outing, with the reinforcement from other mothers who were bringing their children out, parents began to do more on their own.

Perhaps, one of the reasons that the field trips sponsored by the prevention programs made such an impression on parents was that they had not fully realized the positive effects such an event would have on their relationships with their children. Prior to program participation, parents were less aware of their children's abilities and interests. Equally important, before program involvement, parents pointed to television and siblings as the primary sources of cognitive and social stimulation for their children. A high-risk mother of three children, aged 6, 4, and 3 years, one of whom had a learning disability, from FSS, responded,

> Yeah. I'm more creative with the things that I do with my children. Instead, before the program, we watched TV, videos, maybe take them to the playground. We more likely just stayed in the house a lot. Now, I go out a lot with them, one-on-one attention with them out. Like I may have one I may take out of school one day and just shopping and just pal around with me all day. We'll go to the movies or we'll go to the park or we'll go to the Please Touch Museum. I still have my membership there. More so I really get to know my child and how they feel about certain things.

Besides strengthening the parent-child bond, the parents noted the benefits of these outings for their children. They described their children as excited and stimulated. Others noted that their children were easier to deal with once they returned home. They realized that after their children released their energy on these outings, they were tired and were therefore less "rowdy" or "needy."

For some, program participation seemed to transform parenting into a more pleasurable activity, as opposed to a chore. Learning to have fun with their children also appeared in some of the parents' comments describing interactions with their children. A high-risk young mother with two small children, aged 3 and 6, from YSI, explains:

> Yeah. Because before, I took my children to the clinic and we went to the store and basically that was it. I didn't really like to go anywhere because my kids were small, and I felt like I wouldn't be able to have no fun. So then I learned to have fun with my children out. So then we started walking to the playground or going to visit other people with children the same ages as mine.

A mother in treatment for her addiction to drugs who participated in the FSP parenting classes shared about her first experiences taking her children out:

> Yeah. You know. Darn. I ain't never been to a circus and I'm 36 years old. I was always out there hustling and everything. So I don't want to go to the circus but they said, some things they said you have to not be, because I'm a self-centered person, and I have to do something for my children, this is all about breaking this cycle, right? So they give me these tickets to this circus and we go to the circus, which was fun. It was different. I kind of got a little kick out of it because I didn't want everybody to know I never been to the circus. And I didn't know it was like three things that you looked at, and I'm like, and the kids was jumping up and down, they'd never been to a circus either.

By modeling how to have fun with children, the programs significantly changed the way these mothers viewed and interacted with their children.

Increased Educational Activities

In addition to providing more stimulation outside the home, high-risk parents were 3 times more likely than their low-risk counterparts to discuss educational activities in response to the questions, "Have the kind of things you do with your children changed?" For instance, this YSI mother with three small children describes how she changed what she does with her children. She explained,

> Well, now I sit down and read the books every night, I teach my 2-year-old how to tie his shoes and put on her own clothes, and I'll walk to the park and I ask them would they like to go anywhere special. They'll say they want to go to my mom's house, and I'll take them over there to my mom's house. And play around with their little toys and stuff. That's what I do now.

A mother from FSP talked about the activities she did with her 2½-year-old daughter:

> I make her write, get the letters off the refrigerator and have her trace them. I taught her how to spell her name in like a week's time. Then, when I seen that, I was like, Oh we're going to start spelling something now. I'll pronounce things and she'll know them. I'll just be doing stuff with her at home. I just be teaching her. I just be doing stuff that I think they would do. Now, I want to get her to know the letters so I got like a page with just the ABCs and the 123s and so she'll know the numbers and the letters when she goes to school.

The interesting point about this mother is that once she realized how quickly her daughter could learn to spell her name, she became motivated to teach her additional lessons. It appears that high-risk mothers had little comprehension of the importance, and the rewards, of providing stimulation to their children. However, once this behavior was modeled for them, parents initiated these activities on their own.

PROGRAM FACTORS AFFECTING CHANGE

This section seeks to link specific program components with changes in parenting behaviors 2 years following program termination. Ideally, we would examine retention of program benefits separately by site. However, the small sample size for a few of the sites precluded that option. Instead, we focused on specific program characteristics, especially those we found to be influential on parental changes immediately following services, presented in the previous chapter. Relative to other programmatic factors, such as length, type, and number, service frequency had the most powerful effect on change at the end of prevention services. In what follows, we examine characteristics of the services received by the follow-up-sample participants, in concert with postprogram changes, to see if service frequency and referral source produced a sustained impact on information and behavior retention. Even though the other service variables had minimal impact on immediate parenting behavior, we looked at the long-term impact of type and number of services received, as such variables may have had a latent impact on parents.

We augment the discussion of the services received by former participants with their views of how particular service characteristics helped them change their parenting. The study team asked a series of questions designed to assess the participants' experience in the prevention programs, in general, and to understand what types of information parents found most useful, in particular. Two questions, "What do you remember most from the _____ program?" and

"What was most helpful to you?" capture the participants' perceptions of the most memorable features of the programs and what aspects were most helpful.

Services Received by the Follow-up Sample

A thorough inspection of the services actually received by these parents afforded an accurate account of the connection between service characteristics and parental change over time. Our ability to carry out this type of analysis was somewhat limited by the two different data collection strategies employed in the participant impact study. Consequently, the following analysis is based solely on those follow-up participants with complete service use data ($n = 57$).

Follow-up sample members received, on average, 1.4 service contacts per week, with one third remaining in services for longer than 6 months. The majority participated in group-based services, with 68% in counseling, 52% in a combination of center-based and home-based services, and 31% in home-based services only. Over half of the sample was involved with at least three different services; in contrast, only one quarter was involved in a single service. Remarkably, one third of the sample learned about the programs through peer contact, and one quarter came to the programs on their own. Like the demographic characteristics presented earlier, this service profile indicates a very distinct group with more frequent and extensive program contact and greater likelihood of joining programs at the suggestion of a friend than those in the full sample.

Service Frequency

Those participants who engaged in services at least once a week showed sustained improvement on their CAP scores 2 years after program termination, compared to those who received services less than weekly. Although CAP scores improved, service frequency did not have the desired impact on spanking. Parents who spanked their children 6 to 11 times per year at the follow-up interview had received the most intensive services (1.54 contacts per week), although parents who spanked their children monthly received the next most intensive services (1.16 contacts per week), followed by those who never spanked their children (1.05 contacts per week). In contrast, service frequency showed a more linear relationship with how frequently parents insulted their children. Former participants who now refrain from yelling received the most intensive services, compared to those who continue to insult their children. It is interesting that those who insulted their children constantly received services less than once a week. Focusing on the two alternative forms of discipline, denial of privileges and confinement, indicates that those receiving more intensive services were more likely to practice these two behaviors at the follow-up point. Receiving services at least once a week did improve the parent's ability to use alternative forms of discipline, a primary service goal.

Service Type

No one service strategy significantly affected CAP scores or discipline practices at the time of the follow-up interview. Whether a parent attended education workshops, support groups, counseling, or play groups did not seem to influence their long-term parenting. This finding mirrors that of the larger sample.

Referral Source

The source of referral into the prevention programs revealed significant distinctions in long-term parenting practices for this sample. Self-referral and peer referral were the two primary means engaged by this sample to enter prevention services. Fully 50% of the self-referrals improved their CAP scores beyond the programs' end, as compared to only 20% of their peer-referred counterparts. This finding suggests that perhaps individual motivation may indeed be an important ingredient for long-term success. Furthermore, peer referrals reported more regular spanking than self-referrals and were twice as likely to insult their children on a regular basis, as compared to their self-referred counterparts. In fact, peer referrals disciplined much more frequently, so they were also twice as likely to punish their children using denial of privileges than their self-referred counterparts. One interesting difference between these groups concerned their reason for enrolling in parenting programs. Parents referred by peers joined for social reasons, such as meeting other parents or getting a chance to leave their houses. In contrast, self-referred parents sought out these services to help improve their parenting skills.

The Importance of Groups

From the former participants' perspective, eight aspects of the child abuse prevention programs remained important to them 2 years after program termination. These include, in order of frequency, (a) parent groups (21%), (b) information about understanding children (13%), (c) relationships with staff (12%), (d) variety of topics discussed (12%), (e) trips and parties (8%), (f) opportunity for self-analysis (8%), (g) chance for their children to play with other children (7%), and (h) information regarding discipline (5%). A similar pattern emerged in response to what was most helpful, as former participants again cited parent groups (16%), information about discipline (16%), staff (11%), learning patience (8%), counseling (6%), and home visits (5%). In this section, we focus on the most prevalent response—parent groups. Investigating these responses, in conjunction with discipline practices 2 years postprogram, indicated that the reasons former participants gave for finding the groups the most memorable differ by postprogram behavior. Furthermore, this analysis lends some insight into the distinguishing factors between the majority who spanked frequently and the minority who refrained from spanking, even though both engaged in group services.

Seven of the nine prevention programs offered a group service, and 64% of this sample participated in a group service. Parents' viewing the group experience as the most memorable aspect of the programs did not vary with how often they spanked their children. Equal percentages of former participants who spanked frequently and those who never spanked remembered the groups favorably. In contrast, parents who refrained from insulting their children or insulted less than once a month were twice as likely to discuss the groups as the most memorable aspect of the prevention programs.

According to participants, the group format was important because it allowed them the occasion to obtain information from their peers, the chance to see that others shared their frustrations, and the opportunity to involve their children with other children.

Sharing Information With Other Parents

A mother of three children, aged 20, 18, and 13, formerly involved with Crime Prevention's Family Center, discussed the groups as a place to receive input about her individual problems. When she started the group, she was experiencing a lot of "ups and downs" as a single parent to which she attributed having difficulties with her children. In particular, she had been yelling constantly at her 18-year-old daughter, who had an infant of her own. With the group's suggestions, she believed that she was able to handle that situation more effectively. She describes what happened in her group:

> At the time, I was having problems with my daughter, and as a group, we sat and discussed problems the other parents were having with their children. So I got a lot of input and that made me, some of the suggestions made me, a little more I guess patient. Because sometimes, I would just lose it.

A mother of three young children, aged 6, 4, and 3, claimed she is more patient as a result of participating in FSS. At the time of her second interview, she was living with her parents, who contradicted everything she did with her children. Furthermore, two of her children have learning disabilities. She liked the groups because everyone was an equal, explaining,

When I was here, the other mothers and some of the fathers that came, they were real supportive too. No one looked down on each other. No one said, you are a bad parent, or anything like that. They was real supportive and giving you other ideas or whatever.

Another mother of four children, aged 4, 6, 15, and 18, from FSS, stressed the connection between realizing that she was not alone and being able to learn new ways to handle situations with children. She said,

You'll have time to sit back and discuss some of the things that everyday, just something off the top of your mind that you always wondered. And you know what else I liked about it? You get to see that you're not the only one thinking like that. Like if you wanted to choke your child, at least you know others want to do the same thing. And then [staff] say, Okay, this is the way you handle that problem. You all see you're not just the only ones. You not the only one that feels like that. You're not alone in this situation. So she would discuss us on how to handle a problem when it comes up.

Involving the Children

The fact that children were involved in the programs proved to be one of the more important reasons the parents liked the groups. In this regard, parents cited two explanations: a break from their children and the group's assistance with their children's social, emotional, and cognitive development. Although there was not a perfect correlation between these two reasons and parenting practices 2 years later, in general, those showing the least improvement over time were likely to name enjoying a break, whereas those continuing to improve noted the positive effect the groups had on their children. One mother of five children, ranging in age from 3 to 18 years old, who took part in Crime Prevention's program, looked forward each week to the group meeting. She explained,

That we sit around and the parents get a chance to talk, be by themselves and get a chance to bring out things and let out, relax. And we get a chance to be away from the kids because the kids is in one room and the parents is in another room talking about whatever they want to talk about.

In contrast, a mother of three, aged 6, 4, and 3, from FSS, talked about how her child became more outgoing as a result of the group activities:

[My daughter] was real quiet and she was real introverted as far as her personality. She was a really good child. It was just that she was real quiet. And that's been pretty much the way I was when I was young, too. Some of the things that went on around me, I had to stay quiet so I wouldn't get into trouble. And so coming to the program, they helped [my daughter] to open up a little bit. Because she wasn't even playing with the other children. She'll get a toy and go in the corner and go play by herself. Things like that. So she wouldn't have to fight the children for her toy, she didn't have to go through the aggravation. But then, before I graduated from the program, by that time [my daughter] was talking to all the staff members. You couldn't shut her up. It's [my daughter], be quiet, it's nap time. She really broke out of that.

As a participant in Alternatives' parent-child play group, this mother of a 3-year-old also commented on the fact that the parent-child groups allowed her to observe her child interacting with other children. She revealed,

My relatives are like far and away. So this is a good opportunity for me to see him interact with other children and him to get used to playing with children of many ages because it was from infants up to about age 3 and some of them had their older brothers and sisters along.

Although group activity, for the most part, had a limited prolonged impact on parenting practices, the parents themselves appreciated group time. The comments from parents who did not improve suggest that the social aspect of the groups may have been more meaningful to them than any specific parenting information they acquired. In contrast, parents who did improve attempted to put this information to use in addition to appreciating the support.

LESSONS LEARNED

We found great diversity in parenting attitudes and practices 2 years after the programs ended. Roughly 30% displayed continued improvement, 30% persisted in using unhealthy forms of discipline, and the remaining 40% fell somewhere between these two extremes. On the bright side, many parents reported increased involvement with their children, as evidenced by more time spent with their children. These parents considered the group meetings especially useful, a time to garner support for their parenting and to see their children interact with other children. Those who sustained or improved on what they learned from the programs were more likely to have received services weekly and to have sought out the program on their own. Thus, the Penn programs made enduring impressions on some extremely vulnerable families, families generally considered hard to reach and hard to maintain in family support programs.

Unfortunately, not all families achieved this success, as only 30% continued to improve. For some, a child's movement into more active child development stages may have prompted the use of unhealthy discipline strategies. For others, the program information regarding later stages of child development may not have seemed relevant at the time. In the next chapter, we offer some hypotheses for why these gains were not sustained. For now, we return to the positive finding that most parents did, in fact, begin to use alternative forms of discipline. The large percentage of former participants who denied privileges, a figure similar to the percentage for the U.S. public, illustrates this point. However, it appears that rather than applying the more positive forms of discipline as a substitute for spanking or yelling, former participants used them in conjunction with these established behaviors. This change in itself is noteworthy and may indeed be a necessary first stage for high-risk parents to alter their discipline strategies.

Service Providers

- Providers need to be realistic about the types of changes they expect the highest-risk parents to make as a result of supportive services. Our data suggest that understanding the long-term harmful consequences of physical punishment and verbal abuse does not necessarily translate into refraining from these behaviors.

- Services offered at least once a week will yield the greatest long-term impacts on participants. Of the program characteristics we examined, only service frequency could be linked with long-term change. Those who received the most frequent services continued to show a decrease in child abuse potential and verbal abuse.

- Programs should realize that peer-referred families may need extensive support to make sustained parenting changes. Generally, we tend to think that programs that attract peer referrals are successful and effective. Although these programs may have developed an attractive program, our findings suggest many peer-referred parents have joined the program to be with their friends and to enjoy the social aspects of the programs rather than to work on their parenting.

- Family support programs should incorporate some type of group-based services to address the social isolation of parents. Even though participation in group services made minimal inroads on parental use of corporal punishment or swearing, the fact that former participants praised these parenting groups as the most helpful type of intervention offered by prevention programs leads us to believe that such groups serve to keep parents involved in services.

- Child abuse prevention programs addressing corporal punishment need to stress the importance of substituting more healthy forms of discipline for nonhealthy ones. Although the Penn programs were successful in teaching parents to use time out and to talk with their children, they had more limited success in convincing parents not to hit their children.

- Providers and planners should incorporate experiential parent education into services. Parents were quite vocal in describing how fields trips benefited their children and taught the mothers how to negotiate such activities.

Funders and Policymakers

- Follow-up studies should be an integral part of comprehensive program evaluations so that we can begin to build a body of knowledge about the long-term gains of family support programs.

- Funders and policymakers should support programs that target older parents with multiple children. Although it is common for family support interventions, especially those aimed at preventing child abuse, to limit the target population to first-time parents, our findings show that parents with multiple children can also benefit from such services.

Researchers

- Research combining both quantitative and qualitative data produces more valuable information regarding program effects than designs that only incorporate one analytic framework. The quantitative data reveal the amount of impact the program exerted on parents, but the qualitative data can explain why parenting is or is not transformed through participation in a family support program. We urge researchers to incorporate methods to capture the participants' voice in evaluation studies.

CHAPTER 5

Barriers to Parental Change

Parenting seldom occurs in a vacuum. Parents are influenced not only by their personality and experience but also by the people surrounding them, notably family and friends, and by the community in which they live. This ecological perspective (Belsky, 1980; Bronfenbrenner, 1979), with its emphasis on both personal and situational factors that shape parenting behavior, is useful for unraveling the reasons that some parents continue to use harsh discipline practices despite voluntarily engaging in services to alter this behavior. In this chapter, we identify both the internal barriers that prevented parents from implementing less aggressive disciplinary strategies and the external barriers encountered by some as they struggled to maintain the gains they had achieved while receiving services. The participant responses raised two key issues, family criticism and community violence, that need to be addressed explicitly by family support programs to achieve lasting impacts. Last, we explore the meaning of success, from the participant's viewpoint. This line of inquiry demonstrates a considerable gap between program definitions of success and parental views of improvement.

INTERNAL BARRIERS

We first found that ingrained personality factors impeded participant progress. Other studies have acknowledged that personal dysfunction is more common among abusive parents, with such parents exhibiting more depression, lower self-esteem, and poorer impulse control than nonabusive parents (Baumrind, 1992; Cicchetti & Lynch, 1993). For example, abusive parents tend to show greater annoyance and irritation in response to their children's behavior than their nonabusive counterparts (Casanova, Domaniac, McCanne, & Milner, 1992). In fact, abusive parents perceive their children's behavior as more aggressive, intentionally disobedient, and less intelligent than do nonabusive parents. Among the parents who continued to discipline their children frequently and harshly, these same beliefs and risk factors emerged during our interviews. In the following discussion, we restricted our analyses to those parents in the follow-up sample who continued to use aggressive parenting behavior with their children. Specifically, we focused on those 25 parents who reported hitting their children and the 19 parents who reported yelling and swearing at their children monthly (13 of these parents engaged in both).

Physical Discipline as a Means to Maintain Control

Parents who spanked monthly consistently talked about the need to have control of their children. A surprising number discussed this issue in conjunction with the discipline questions or in conjunction with what they wanted to change about their parenting. An FSS mother who relies on multiple techniques provided a useful illustration. She first discussed how the program staff explained and demonstrated what to do, saying,

> When children want their way, they [staff] say, "No, you can't have your way," and make them sit down. Or they don't want to listen or they want to get up and throw tantrums, you know kids do that sometimes, and when they do that, they [staff] put them in the corner.

In response to how she handled a similar episode, she said she would take a belt and hit her children until they calmed down. She further believes that she has to tap her children with a belt every once in a while to keep them under control. When asked what she learned from the program, she responded,

> I'm learning how to put them under control. That's the main thing I wanted. Before, when everything was out of control, I just let them went wild and stuff, and I let them rip and run, rip and run. And they got on my nerves and screaming and I get the belt and want to smack them all around.

Furthermore, when parents were asked what they would like to change about their parenting, "having more control" emerged as one of the prevalent responses, especially among those who spanked frequently, as two thirds of them gave this response. Based on their descriptions of having more control, parents wanted children to obey them and not cause raucous scenes at home or in public. Such a definition suggests that parental need for control may be related to self-esteem issues, with quiet, orderly children representing successful parenting.

Parental Inconsistency

An additional characteristic common to parents who spanked frequently was their use of inconsistent discipline. Many attempted to enforce a nonphysical form of discipline only to eventually give in to their children's demands. The next time the child acted out in a similar fashion, the frustrated mother reverted back to physical discipline, with the belief that alternative forms of discipline were not effective. This response may indicate poor impulse control on the part of the mother, as the desire for immediate results appeared to supersede the willingness to try out alternative discipline strategies.

A mother of four children provides an example of "giving in" as she describes what her 2-year-old does that "gets on her nerves." She responds,

> His crying for the bottle. That's one main thing with him. I'll just give it to him or I'll tell him he can't have it. Sometimes, I'll have to smack his hands because he'll go get the broom and watch where I put it at [the bottle] and he'll try to get it down. So sometimes I'll smack his hands and set him down and he just cries. But eventually it gets me tired out, so I give it to him.

Even more disturbing is her behavior toward her 4-year-old. She remarks,

> I don't know. She'll take and hit one of the other ones. They will be sitting there looking at TV and she'll take and just jump off and go smack one of them or hit one of them. And sometimes I just yell at her and sometimes I make them hit her back and then I send her up to her room.

Besides taking minimal action to resolve the problem of the 4-year-old hitting her siblings, this mom reinforces to her children that hitting is an acceptable form of dealing with conflict by "making" them hit the 4-year-old back.

Another mother talks about letting her small children, a 2-year-old and an 11-month-old, get away with things, within the context of how often she hits her children. She explains,

> It's not even a lot. I'll say once in a while they get a smack on their hands. Most of the time they jus do what they want and get away with it, she does because she's the oldest, but the little one, she doesn't really do too much anyway.

It's not surprising that this mother remained unconvinced about what she learned from the parenting program. She revealed,

Like she'll [staff] say, don't hit the kids, but they have to be taught obedience and they have to know that and they have to be smacked on the hand and that's what I do. The program doesn't say that. They say, "Don't do it, sit down and talk to them." Sometimes talking doesn't work. So what else are you supposed to do?

Emotional Detachment

A smaller group of mothers tended to inordinately ignore their children, perhaps as a result of clinical depression, though this was not documented by the Penn programs. During the interviews, they left the impression of being completely detached from their children, almost as if their children were invisible. Again, for these mothers, using alternative forms of discipline might be difficult, as they demand a more intimate level of interaction, such as talking with the child, than does hitting. Indeed, these were the mothers who claimed that their children's desire for attention was a behavior deserving physical punishment.

The responses from a former Philadelphia Society mother provided an example of parents who remained emotionally detached from their children, affording an important picture of how parents did not change. This mother began service in her early 20s with only one child. By the follow-up interview, she had two additional children. Her responses throughout her interview indicate minimal interaction with her children. In response to how she has changed her behavior with her children, she responded,

Before the program, I used to holler at them, throw shoes at them, beat them, anything, as long as they shut up. Now, instead of hollering at them, I just talk to them. Instead of beating them, I just talk to them, please stop. Like how they say, instead of yelling at them, just let them play and play until they get tired of playing. So I let them play and play until they just fall out.

Despite this comment, she reported hitting and yelling at her children monthly. It appears that her main goal was to have her children leave her alone, as she has substituted letting them play until they are exhausted for constant physical discipline. Furthermore, when asked how she would deal with an infant crying in the night, she said, "I go to sleep first." Her response differs dramatically from that given by the rest of the sample. Most mothers said something about checking to see if the baby was all right, holding the baby, rocking the baby, and so forth.

In the end, many of these parents' discipline practices remained inconsistent, undoubtedly leaving their children confused about what behaviors were acceptable. It is important to recognize that the majority of parents come into the prevention programs with this negative, circular interaction between their children and themselves already firmly in place. Such continued erratic parental behavior probably triggered a cycle in which the child challenges the parents, the parent views the child as bad or unruly and ends up hitting the child, the child perceives that he or she is a problem, continues to act out, and so forth. In these situations, family support programs need to remind parents that inconsistent discipline will only make the situation worse.

EXTERNAL BARRIERS

Parents revealed two external issues that hindered their ability to fully incorporate what they had learned in the Penn programs into their everyday lives with their children. These two issues, criticism from friends and the pervasiveness of violent neighborhoods, are part of the ecosystem in which parenting occurs. Although neighborhoods now are recognized as important contextual factors for understanding child maltreatment, it remains unclear exactly how neighborhood conditions affect parenting (National Research Council, 1993). The follow-up sample's comments shed some light on the ways such influences affected their long-term ability to improve their roles as parents.

Barriers Imposed by Family and Peers

During our interviews, we asked the question, "Has anyone ever criticized you about the way you deal with your children?" If the parent said yes, we went on to ask the source and nature of the criticism. This question's initial intent was to determine, indirectly, whether the parent had ever been reported to Child Protective Services. The parents responded in ways we had not anticipated. To our surprise, one third of the parents replied that their peers and family members considered them too lenient with their children. Only 2% had been told they were maltreating their children, 9% had been criticized as too strict, and 37% of the parents had received no criticism. Criticism came primarily from family members (38%), though 14% of these remarks came from nonrelatives, and 11% of the comments came from both of these sources. Therefore, it became evident that for at least one third of the sample, the information and skills taught by prevention programs differed dramatically from how many around them parented. The use of physical discipline was especially at issue.

To date, research has not clarified the relationship between informal social networks and parenting practices (National Research Council, 1993). These responses suggested that lack of positive reinforcement from peers helped erode any strides in new behavior achieved among our follow-up sample. We decided to investigate this issue more thoroughly by asking the former participants to talk about how they felt about this criticism and to what degree it impeded their ability to use what they learned from the programs. Furthermore, we obtained additional information about how family and friends dealt with their own children.

Of the follow-up sample, 80% reported that they had been criticized about their parenting. Most of the criticism came from family members and close friends who believed the former participants were too lenient with their children. Of those who spanked or insulted their children routinely, 32% responded that they were told by both family members and friends that they were too lenient. It is interesting that this group was composed primarily of the former participants who added a positive discipline practice, such as privilege denial and confinement, to their disciplinary actions even though they continued to spank often. Moreover, 40% of those who spanked frequently had never received criticism about their parenting, implying that their parenting behavior represented the norm in their particular peer group.

Family members usually thought that parents should hit their children more often. The following quote from a former Philadelphia Society participant who rarely spanked or insulted her children provides an example of the type of comments her family made to her. In this case, her brother-in-law, who beats his own children constantly, was the source of criticism. She described their disagreement in these terms:

> *Respondent:* It didn't make me no difference. I told him they can be spoiled as long as he don't touch them. If they ain't your child, you don't touch them. He told me that if they are upstairs jumping on that bed, he's going to go up there and beat all of them. He's talking about my sister's kids, his kids. His kids and my kids. He says he's going to go up there and beat all of them.
>
> *Interviewer:* Does he beat his kids?
>
> *Respondent:* Yes. He beats them all the time. My kids over at the house jumping, they was all upstairs playing, I guess they was making a lot of noise, probably jumping on the bed I think. If they are up there jumping on the bed, I'm going to go up there and beat every kid that's up there. I said, You'd better not touch mine. I said, we'd be up there fighting.

Such familial criticism is not limited only to participants with the greatest risk of spanking their children. The story of a mother of an 8-year-old and an 11-year-old exemplified the types of disparaging remarks parents received from family members. This mother, who spanked once a year, was chastised by both her mother and her husband. She speaks of her mother's commentary:

> It's like, she just shakes her head and sometimes she'll say to me, My kids never behaved that way, a good smack will do it. But then if you were to do it, she'll be like, well, then she'll go over and pamper them and I'll say, Mom, I can't do that, I

just punished him for what he did. And if I leave and I leave him there, or sometimes it's both of them, I'll hear, Well, he was so good, I walked him down to Waldeman's and bought him an ice cream and a candy bar. It's things like that, oh God.

Furthermore, she goes on to say that these criticisms sometimes made it difficult to use what she learned from the prevention programs, especially if her son's behavior was severe. More important, these comments make her doubt her own judgment and undermine her self-esteem.

Those former participants who resided with their families, as 18% of this sample did, faced even greater challenges to altering their parenting behavior. In many cases, other family members go beyond criticism and directly interfere with parenting.

They wouldn't try to talk to them first, they wouldn't try to calm them down first, they wouldn't try to see what was on the child's mind, why they are acting like this, ask them some questions.

This mother and her three small children, two of whom are developmentally delayed, lived with her parents who made it particularly difficult for her to attempt new behavior with her children. Her parents thought differently about raising children than she did, and they reminded her constantly. She reports,

They will say things like, I'm too hard on them, or they will turn around and say I'm too soft on them. If I don't crack down on them now, they will be in jail and whose fault would that be, it would be your fault because you didn't discipline them in the proper way. . . . It makes me feel like an inadequate mother.

She later goes on to give a concrete example of her parents' interference by describing what happens when it is time for the children to go to bed, saying,

Oh, that's crying, I don't want to go to sleep, I'm not tired. They will scream and holler just so my parents will come upstairs, and then my parents will yell at me and they will see my parents yelling at me and they will start yelling at me and so it's like real difficult at night.

Another participant, also living with her family, told a similar story about her conflict with her family members and how it disrupted what she was trying to do with her children. In describing a typical day at her house she said,

It's hectic. Every day, yes, it's hectic. Me and my mother arguing a lot, then she starts arguing with me and then I start arguing with the kids and it just goes to my sister, and it's really hectic every day, it's like arguing and fussing, arguing and fussing. The kids are just getting tired of it. [My daughter] has told me, I wish you all would stop. She got mad at my mother because me and her were upstairs kind of fighting, and she told my mother, she said, I'll kill you. She's getting tired of hearing her talk to me the way she does, hit me, because she understands what's going on. She doesn't like it at all. But it's mostly verbal abuse and a lot of hollering and screaming. But that happens every day. That's why I go to counseling because otherwise I wouldn't be able to deal with my problems. So I have to seek some help.

Criticism from participants' friends about their new parenting approaches proved to be equally harsh and influential. Again, these comments revealed that many parents resided in social networks where aggressive parenting practices were the norm. Although half of the participants claimed that they were not concerned with what their family and friends had to say about their newly acquired parenting style, their ambivalence came through in some of their responses. A former Philadelphia Society participant remarked that she had been told by her male friend, brother, and mother that she "spoils her children" and "lets them have their way too often." In response to whether this hindered her ability to apply what she learned from the prevention programs, she replied,

> Yeah. But, no, I don't, it doesn't worry me, because I know how I used to feel when my mother used to beat me with an extension cord. She gave us a lot, and I have a problem with that.

In contrast, 19% of the former participants said that others' comments did bother them and therefore made it difficult to consistently maintain what they learned. For example, an FSP mother who frequently spanked and was also reproached as too lenient, admits that when pressured by her friends, she would hit her child. She says,

> It's real different because it's like before I learned it, it was like if your child misbehaves, you spank him and put him in his room or whatever. And I be around a lot of my girlfriends and they be like, don't sit there and talk to him and he's going to do it again and you shouldn't do that. So it's like being the oddball. And then I feel a lot of times I have caught myself saying, Well it's like they are putting a lot of pressure on me and so while I'm with them, I'll beat his behind and put him in the corner and then I'll try at home to do what I feel is the right way. So it's real hard.

It is interesting that this mother did not change her behavior completely, only when she was with her friends. However, her inconsistency toward her son no doubt caused him confusion and may eventually override the positive actions she took with him at home.

Given the intensity of the comments from the significant individuals in their lives, it became more evident why some parents had difficulty using and sustaining new parenting behaviors. Simply, they received very little support and many negative comments. Prevention programs could play a stronger role in deterring some of this resistance or, at a minimum, in preparing their participants for a negative reaction from those close to them. Furthermore, the fact that a notable percentage of former participants who spanked frequently reported no criticism is also disturbing. Apparently, this group receives minimal encouragement to change their behavior. Instead, their social networks support the very behaviors most parents, program providers, and policymakers seek to change.

COMMUNITY VIOLENCE

A substantial number of former participants, especially those from Philadelphia Society, FSS, APM, Congreso, and YSI reside in neighborhoods fraught with gang violence. Of the 56 former participants interviewed at the 2-year time point, fully 78% shared that worrying about violence consumed a lot of their time. In particular, two thirds worried that one of their own children would be harmed. Although we do not have enough data to claim a direct causal relationship between community violence and excessive physical discipline, these two factors appear related in this sample. Of those parents who were concerned about violence, over half spanked their children frequently.

The participants' descriptions of their neighborhoods illustrated the magnitude of frightening behavior occurring in the same space where they were raising their children. A former FSS participant who spanked and yells monthly described her children's world and her own as limited by the violence, saying,

> I worry about it, but if I ever move, which I will, I'm just going to get me some bars put on my windows and get a bunch of locks on my door. I do worry about their safety. They can't play out in the street. That's why we're kind of scared to go out, I'm kind of scared. I don't mean to hold them back, but I just don't want them to get hurt.

She goes on to say,

> I turn away from it. Like I said, I lock myself up my own little world and I just turn away. I don't worry about it or nothing. I don't go out too much or date too much because I don't trust anybody. That's a problem. If I could, I would. But it's just hard for me to trust anybody now.

A former Philadelphia Society mother described how the influx of crack into the neighborhood dramatically changed the quality of life, claiming that the addicts will "do anything they have to do to get the money for that drug." She explains,

It's definitely that crack. You can go into some neighborhoods and like say 10 years ago, it was much different. The houses was maintained well. Now they are letting the houses fall apart. I mean you have the dealers out all times of the night, so that draws that type of crowd and that's what causes most of the violence because these people are craving for this drug and they are doing whatever they have to do to get it. It's just the root of a whole lot of our problems.

Another Philadelphia Society former participant who spanked and insulted her children monthly, volunteered her version of the neighborhood in response to what she worried about most for her children, saying,

Just violence. Out there where I'm at, it's violence. As soon as the sun goes down, you start hearing gunshots. I'm like, Oh my God. And my baby, he thinks they are firecrackers all the time when he hears them. We hear the firecrackers? Yeah, I hear the firecrackers. It's real wild up that way.

Strategies Used to Protect Children

Former participants named four specific strategies they employed to help protect their children: (a) limiting the child's boundaries (21%), (b) talking with children about the violence (19%), (c) always knowing the child's whereabouts (19%), and (d) keeping the children in the house (16%). Such strategies mirror those used by parents in other urban environments (Garbarino, Dubrow, Kostelny, & Pardo, 1992).

The Philadelphia Society participant who spoke about the impact of crack reported that she talked with her children about the situation. She explained,

I don't hide it from them. I tell about it and the outcome and I show them. The next day I'll say for example, like if it's somebody I know, I will say, You see that person. I knew her a long time ago. She was this way then and look at her now. It has them out there robbing their mother, their father, they are killing one another.

A former participant from Crime Prevention also talked with her 12-year-old daughter, on an ongoing basis, about avoiding violence:

I was telling her, You see what can happen when you get in trouble. Maybe she took it in, maybe she didn't. I don't know. But I keep telling her to stay away from. I was telling her Sunday, stay away from trouble, they will cut you or shoot you now. They don't fight with their little hands no more.

Another Philadelphia Society participant with small children also talked with her children about what is going on. She said,

Like I say, I tell them about it and the little ones, they basically are in the house with me. They are with me most of the time. When I'm not at work, they are home. When I'm off work, they travel with me. I try to keep them close to me at all times. I don't like to let them go out a lot by theirselves. Like in the summertime when they do go out, I'm out there with them. I don't allow them to go out until I come too.

Other parents set boundaries as to how far their children can venture when they are outside playing. A Philadelphia Society former participant explained, "I feel like, well don't go past [a neighbor's] porch. If anything was to happen and they was down there that she would put them in her house, stuff like that." For other mothers, they restrict the time of day in which the children can go outside. The mother from FSS quoted about her fear at the beginning of this chapter said,

Most of the time, we go out in the mornings. So we don't go out at night, not at all. If I go to the movies, it would have to be about 2 or 3 o'clock or something like that. At night, I don't like bringing them out at night.

A high-risk mother from FSS who spanked and yelled monthly restricted her children's boundaries by limiting with whom they can play. She explained,

Yes. For instance, my children don't play with no kids on the block because they are very violent, and I'm already having problems with them now. If they be exposed to even more violence, who knows how rough they can be in school. So they don't really play, they play with the people that we know in the hallway and other children that's not on the hall but that I can see are not very violent, maybe they can show a positive look on things for them so they don't have to be so negative and so hard on other people.

When asked what she meant by some of the kids in the neighborhood being violent, she replied,

The sayings they use, how they steal things to be so young, they talk about sex and things like that. My kids don't know anything about it now. I don't want them to know anything about it right now anyway, not unless they ask me a question and then I will answer it. But the street stuff isn't healthy.

A high-risk mother from APM who reported never spanking and never yelling at her children talked about how she never leaves her children. She said,

Yes, because I can never leave them. When I first moved into this house, I could sit on the balcony and watch them. But now I can't even let them go out on their bicycles for the fear they might be hit by a bullet, or that someone comes and takes the children away. There is too much violence.

Exposure to Violence

Former participants' worries were not unfounded. Over one half of the participants or their children have witnessed a violent episode, generally a shooting. Furthermore, the violence was continual, as one quarter of this sample was exposed to a violent episode at least once a week. When asked how they thought such exposure affected their children, over half said that the incident made their children afraid. For example, a high-risk mother from FSS who spanked and insulted her child monthly talked about her son's behavior after he witnessed a shooting outside of his house:

> Uh huh. My son, he witnessed somebody getting shot outside. He was right in that little area and thank God it wasn't him that got shot. The guy got shot in his side. He said it just scared him and he really was shook up for like a week I think.

After seeing this, her son ran upstairs and "He just kept talking about it, talking about it and walking back and forth." According to his mother, this behavior continued for about a week. Now, she said, "He watches over his back, I know that." As to how the mother responded to this incident, she said, "I just said, I want to get out of here, I don't want to be around here. It's too much."

Another mother talks about how the lifestyle associated with addiction is visible to her children even in their own building. She remarked,

> Using drugs. I think that's a violence. My daughter witnessed a blind man shooting up drugs in the hallway. That's just constantly, people in the hall smoking their crack pipes. That stuff goes down in kids' systems and that's just horrible. I just got to keep telling the kids you can't go in the hallway and play because things just happening out there. Bad things.

A mother from Philadelphia Society talked about how she and her two children, 7 years old and 5 years old, recently witnessed a shooting as they were coming out of the day care center. When all of the day care workers ran back inside to avoid gunfire, everyone, including this mother and her two children, had to stay for a while until the shooting stopped before they could go home. She reported that her son got scared, but it did not affect her daughter at all. Her son is still scared, and his mother thinks that television adds to the problem. She talks about how she handled this situation, saying,

> He hears strange sounds on TV, and he tells me those are the same sounds I hear in here, and I try to explain to him it could be me, it could be a mouse, it could be the cat. I mean I try to explain to him like I don't ever want to talk to him about supernatural things or anything like that. I don't let him watch that on TV. I was afraid of the devil when I was little, and that's something he shouldn't be worrying about. I

explain things without supernatural happenings. So I try to give him a realistic explanation like why he hears the sounds and it could be the heater.

Another Philadelphia Society mother discussed how she talks to her 7-year-old son who has witnessed violence and is very concerned about being shot himself:

> Well, violence already had affected him because he was already gone through this thing with him worrying about violence because the guns. People are shooting all the time, so he was worrying about him getting shot. Now I talk to him about that because it wasn't that he was thinking about it, it's more than that at 6 years old. He's now 7. He was worrying about that. And it kind of hurt me, but . . .

This mother says that she tried to talk to her son about the incident, saying,

> I said basically a lot of God, things about God and then when you see them drawing the guns, don't stay around and have a conversation, you get out of Dodge and just some Bible tips because he has to stay on his own. He likes to go outside. He's growing up, and I can't stop that. That's reality.

In response to how she felt about these circumstances, she related,

> I don't like it. I'm not pleased. But I do have to deal with it. So I deal with it. That's why I do not take my children for granted. I appreciate them because they may not be there tomorrow. Even if I holler at them, at least I know that was a good hollering, or a good butt beating, or spanking, or whatever you call it. That's why our relationship is the way it is because I understand there is no guarantee.

PARENTAL DEFINITION OF CHANGE

The follow-up interviews showed us that understanding parents' frames of reference regarding what types and how much punishment is acceptable plays a central role in determining how parents gauge their own progress. Throughout the interviews, we asked participants to describe their own changes in parenting relative to how they behaved toward their children before participating in services. In addition, the study team inquired about any differences that might exist between the way the former participants parent in relation to the way they were parented.

Most parents who spanked or insulted their children monthly (84%) asserted that their discipline practices had improved as a result of participating in the prevention programs. A mother described how she treated her 2-, 9-, and 11-year-old sons before going to the prevention programs. She disclosed,

Oh, I could not help it. I hit them. I hit them. It wasn't that I wanted to beat them. It was that I did not know how to punish them. In that period, I hit them with whatever was nearby, with a broom, with a frying pan. And I hit them, I gave them blows that could have really hurt them. I could have killed them. I would get them by the neck, I was desperate. That was before we were given help by the program. Thank God for the program because I would never have been helped without it.

In response to what she does now when her sons fight, she attempts to separate the boys and to calm them down by talking and reasoning with them. These new methods have proven effective for her. She further explained how her sons responded to this new behavior, saying,

But it's not like it was before. Not anymore. It's not a big problem anymore. They are getting along like normal boys. But before it was different. Before it was ugly. The younger one grabbed a scissors and went after the other one. It was different how they used to treat each other. Very ugly.

This description reveals how a cycle of violence can be interrupted by changing the parent's behavior. Most likely, her sons' violence toward each other reflected her violence toward them. By modeling less aggressive parental behavior herself, she provided her sons with less incentive to use violence.

Though continuing to yell monthly, a former participant reported no longer insulting her grandchild. Left with the responsibility of raising her 11-year-old granddaughter because her own daughter (the child's mother) was on drugs, this former participant spoke about her frustration in dealing with the child. She said that she no longer had the patience to raise children. Consequently, before attending Crime Prevention, the grandmother would allow the granddaughter "to get away with things." This situation led the grandmother to constantly insult her granddaughter. After having the group's support, especially from other grandmothers, she described how she changed the way she talked to her granddaughter, saying, "I don't have to be screaming at her all the time. And I stopped telling her she was like her mother. I just let her know she's herself."

Also with the help of the group, the grandmother learned to set limits and give the grandchild some responsibility, two behaviors she was using at the time of her interview. Nonetheless, this grandmother yelled at her granddaughter monthly, even though what she says is not as damaging as it was previously.

The other point of reference from which former participants gauged their progress was the way they were raised. Although the intergenerational transmission of abuse continues to be a popular explanation for parental behavior toward their children, the empirical results are mixed. Retrospective studies indicate a range of intergenerational maltreatment from 7% (Gil, 1970), to 30% (Kaufman & Zigler, 1987), to 70% (Egeland & Jacobvitz, 1984). How this process occurs, however, remains a subject for debate. For example, the role of social learning and bonding in the intergenerational transmission of abuse is not clear.

In the follow-up sample, 68% claimed that they parent their children differently than they were reared. Specifically, 41% reported that they hit their children less than they were hit growing up, in large part, as a result of the prevention programs. The following excerpt from a woman who experienced several different foster-care placements as a child demonstrates her point of reference as she discussed her mother:

> She was pretty rough on me. She like abused me a little bit. I never did cross her because she used to hit me with a cord naked, and I never hit my kids with a cord naked. The only time I ever, I went downstairs and he was showing off in church, and I went for the shoe and I pulled his pants down and I spanked his little naked butt. But I wouldn't take my kids' clothes off and beat them with a cord. Not naked, I don't think that's, that's mistreating. I call that abused. I was a little abused, but I wouldn't abuse them like that because I love my kids and I try to set limits.

This woman had had one of the most difficult childhoods of the entire sample, though she may well be similar to other mothers involved with Child Protective Services. She presented an interesting perspective, as she said she loves her children yet she spanked her child in public for common child behavior. In her mind, both are true. This example also illustrates her "internal yardstick" or how she decides what behaviors are abusive. From her perspective, as long as she does not use an extension cord, she is not abusive.

It also is important to recognize that the divergence in behavior from the way they were raised was true for those parents who do not spank, as well. Many of the parents who do not currently use spanking as a form of discipline were themselves hit as children. Unlike those who spanked monthly, these parents have been able to break the cycle. Indeed, some participants sought out the prevention programs precisely because they were hit as children and were afraid they would imitate their parents. For example, a former participant in Alternatives' parent-child play group who never spanked her 3-year-old son, stated,

> As far as our discipline as children, it was a game to my sister. But I remember getting spanked, but I always knew I was spanked and there was a reason for it. But I remember being embarrassed by it, and I certainly didn't want [my 13-year-old son] to feel that. And the time-out program I felt was very good that they did do that because you do hear so much about child abuse these days. And I had always resolved that I wouldn't spank a child, but at that point, I didn't have a solid idea of how I would avoid doing that and what the alternative would be to that. Sitting them in the corner, you wanted to have something in there to take its place because you certainly want them to know that their behavior was not acceptable.

Last, though many parents continued to spank and yell often, they also still wished to change that behavior. The fact that the prevention programs affected the way these parents think about their children's discipline is evident. The following quote from an FSP participant, mother of five children, who yells at her children 6 to 11 times per year, illustrates this point. In response to how she had changed, she noted,

> Like hollering. There is a difference between stern and hollering. So I learned to be stern, but I try not to holler. I'm ain't saying I'm totally. I try not to. But when I do, I be conscious of it. After I do it, then my conscience kicks in and says that was wrong, you don't do it that way. Before, I be like hollering and I ain't give a darn. But now it's different.

When asked what aspects of their parenting persistently concern them, one fifth of those who yell monthly wanted to yell less and one third of those spanking monthly wished they could stop spanking. Though their behavior has not changed, these parents nonetheless expressed a desire to do so. This constitutes a clear change in attitude, which might translate into sustained behavioral change with additional prevention services.

LESSONS LEARNED

For many families, especially those living in unsafe communities, the desire to provide a more nurturing home environment was offset by the daily realities of life. Parents struggled to implement the lessons they learned from the Penn programs, often thwarted by the attitudes of friends and family and the need to keep their children safe from harm. Through our interviews with parents, we became aware of these obstacles to long-term change and so offer the following suggestions to strengthen support services.

Service Providers

- A significant proportion of staff time needs to be allocated to the topic of discipline, as our data suggest that changing disciplinary practices is an uneven and long-term process. Typically, prevention programs cover a number of topics, with discipline usually taking up one session. Even though several programs used so-called state-of-the-art approaches, highly motivated parents still described difficulty applying the newly acquired information. Philadelphia Society used the MELD program, which involves meeting over a 2-year period; discipline is one of the topics covered. FSS and Alternatives featured parent-child play groups.

- Programs should provide an opportunity for parents to practice new discipline techniques while they are still in the program. By having participants report back to the group or staff about how a particular discipline technique worked, parents would have the chance to talk specifically about their frustrations over their children's behavior. Staff and other parents could give concrete suggestions as well as encouragement regarding real incidents. Role playing or similar types of experiential learning could be incorporated into family support curriculums. Providers also should devote several sessions to discussing ways to confront criticism from others, especially criticism encouraging spanking.

• Some parents might benefit from more intensive psychiatric services. The parents who sought greater control over their children or saw their children's actions as directed toward them may need more in-depth services than voluntary family support programs can provide. For these families, it may be important to develop close working relationships with community-based mental health providers.

• Prevention programs need to address the impact of community violence on parents and children. For example, programs could provide parents with examples of how to talk to their children about witnessing negative activities. Programs should also include support groups for children to talk about their own experiences with violence.

Funders and Policymakers

• A comprehensive policy for confronting child abuse and other negative outcomes for children must acknowledge and address the neighborhood and contextual factors parents confront as they raise their children. We believe that without strategies designed to promote community improvements, placing a well-designed family support program into a chaotic and dangerous neighborhood will achieve few sustained impacts.

Researchers

• Our data highlight the sometimes tenuous link between child-rearing attitudes and actual parenting practices. Even though punitive attitudes were reduced, many parents still employed harsh discipline methods. We believe the field would benefit from longitudinal studies that investigate how and when changes in parenting attitudes translate to changes in practices.

• As we have seen, long-term program success is influenced by a number of factors, including the parent's motivation, the provider's skill, the support from the surrounding network of friends and family, and community resources. Outcome evaluations should incorporate methodology that can assess the influence of each of these ecological levels.

CHAPTER 6

Keys to Engaging Families in Services

Child abuse prevention programs often seem like a good idea to everyone except high-risk mothers.

—Barth et al. (1986, p. 104)

As the opening quote illustrates, most family support programs around the country struggle with the problem of how to reach eligible families and keep them involved with services for the program's duration (Clinton, 1992; Lyons-Ruth, Connell, Grunebaum, & Botein, 1990; Marcenko & Spence, 1994; Olds & Kitzman, 1993; Ramey et al., 1992; Seitz et al., 1985; Siegel, Bauman, Schaefer, Saunders, & Ingram, 1980). Any program's impact is limited to the number of people it touches. Unless a sufficient proportion of the target population can be reached and served, aggregate improvements in rates of child abuse, family functioning, and health status indicators will not be achieved (Barth et al., 1986; Daro & McCurdy, 1994; Gomby et al., 1993; Olds & Kitzman, 1993). If parents believe such services will produce few benefits for their families, then even the most effective programs will fail to achieve notable gains. And because families most in need of services are the ones most likely to avoid these programs (Daro, 1988; Larner et al., 1992; Nagy, Leeper, Hullet-Robertson, & Northrup, 1992), a number of at-risk children will be left without much hope for the future. These issues have implications beyond the family support field: Diverse services, such as substance abuse treatment programs, counseling services, work training programs, and therapeutic services for abusing parents, all grapple with the problem of engaging and retaining their target populations.

Successfully enticing parents into attending a family support program presents the first hurdle for program providers (Gabinet, 1979). Most of the research reporting program success in enrolling parents documents relatively high refusal rates, ranging from 8% (Marcenko & Spence, 1994) to 20% of parents declining services (Hawaii Department of Health, 1992; Liaw & Brooks-Gunn, 1994; NCPCA, 1996; Olds et al., 1986; Siegel et al., 1980). Some evidence also suggests that a substantial portion of parents who initially agree to services (15%-17%) will drop out within the first few weeks of enrollment without ever participating in the program (Marcenko & Spence, 1994; Myers-Walls, Elicker, & Bandyck, 1997; NCPCA, 1996).

Even after successful recruitment, programs confront the challenge of retaining these parents in service (Barth et al., 1986; Daro & McCurdy, 1994; Gabinet, 1979; Larner et al., 1992). Programs may initially attract families only to find that parents tend to come and go over the course of the service cycle. Some families attend one or two sessions and then fail to return, others engage sporadically, and a third group actively participates for an extended period of time before departing the program. Voluntary programs offering longer-term services are especially vulnerable to these kinds of attrition, as demonstrated by the number of evaluations reporting drop-out rates of 25% or more by the end of the first year of services (Clinton, 1992; Hardy & Streett, 1989; Nagy et al., 1992; NCPCA, 1996). In contrast, a handful of programs report very low rates of attrition (Bryce, Stanley, & Garner, as cited in Olds & Kitzman, 1993; Olds et al., 1986; Winters-Smith & Larner, 1993).

The family support field has started to probe engagement issues (Herzog, Cherniss, & Menzel, 1986; O'Leary, Shore, & Wieder, 1984; Powell, 1984; Spoth, Redmond, Hockaday, & Shin, 1996); however, most studies have been limited to identifying demographic characteristics related to program involvement. Through the Penn Initiative, we had the opportunity to take a more comprehensive look at these issues. In addition to investigating whether parents who left the programs had a different demographic and risk profile than those who stayed, we also interviewed a subset of parents themselves to find out what attracted them to the programs in the first place and why they remained involved over time.

Developing a fuller understanding of why parents decide to leave or to stay in support programs is crucial if we wish to design truly supportive intervention efforts. By identifying what types of families pose a greater risk of dropping out, program providers can devise ways to restructure services to reduce attrition. Determining whether parents who leave or refuse services are the most in need of support or already have their own support network in place can help program designers and policymakers target intervention efforts toward those families most likely to benefit from parent support programs. In this chapter, we discuss some of the key determinants of program involvement that emerged as a result of our analyses and their implications from both program and policy perspectives.

METHOD AND PARTICIPANTS

Typically, researchers statistically compare program completers to noncompleters in an effort to distinguish the key markers of program involvement. Though such information cannot tell us why certain parents are more or less active in voluntary services, it is a useful first step for differentiating the types of parents who elect to disengage from services prematurely. We made such comparisons between the 371 parents who completed services and the 295 parents who dropped out. To get at the reasons for parental participation, we also explored the more informative "why" question: Why do parents choose to participate or leave family support services? We interviewed 67 former program participants 2 years after program termination to find out why they sought out the prevention programs and what they found most valuable. Though this follow-up sample is relatively small and not necessarily representative of all those who have contact with prevention services,[1] their perceptions complement the quantitative comparisons and help to form some consistent themes about ways to improve recruitment and retention efforts, especially among high-risk parents.

This chapter first identifies some common demographic factors that characterized dropouts across the programs, confirming that higher-risk families tend to depart services earlier than lower-risk families. To flesh out why such families dropped out, our discussion weaves in responses from the smaller follow-up sample to these questions:

What kind of help were you looking for when you came to the program?

What helped you the most?

What do you remember the most about the program?

Have you told family or friends about the _____ program? If so, what did you tell them?

The first three questions generated typical reasons for participation, such as "to learn about parenting," found on many consumer satisfaction, closed-ended surveys. The responses to the final question were more instructive, as the phrasing of this question prompted a naturalistic account of participants' perceptions of the programs.

Similar to the studies described earlier, the Penn programs experienced a rather substantial amount of attrition during the course of services (see

Figure 6.1). Close to 35% of the families dropped out of services prematurely. Though most of these dropouts ended services of their own accord ($n = 254$), the programs themselves also terminated a small number of families from services because the family was referred to Child Protective Services or could no longer be helped by the program (5%, $n = 41$). In contrast, 44% of families either completed the service cycle or had achieved their service goals at the time program involvement ended. Nearly one quarter of the families (21%) were still receiving services at the study's conclusion.

The findings presented in Table 6.1 reinforce the notion that families who refuse or subsequently drop out of voluntary support programs are more at risk for parenting difficulties than those who follow through with services (Daro, 1988; Larner et al., 1992; Nagy et al., 1992). As we expected, both the staff's assessment of parenting risk and the parent's own self-report revealed that dropouts did indeed possess a greater need for parental education and support than completers. On average, dropouts were assessed as displaying more risk factors and adult functioning problems than program completers. For instance, non-completers more often exhibited an inaccurate sense of the child's needs and a cursory knowledge of child development than completers did. As troubling, program dropouts also entertained greater doubts about their self-worth and showed a marked tendency to devalue their capabilities in comparison to parents who completed services.

In terms of maltreatment risk, staff appraised dropouts as significantly more likely than persisters to engage in two forms of neglect: inadequate supervision and medical neglect. Furthermore, parents exiting services early scored 234 on the entry CAP as compared to 205 for those who remained ($p < .001$). Thus, the typical noncompleter ranked in the highest risk category of CAP (i.e., scored more than 214), whereas completers displayed a moderate potential for physical abuse (Milner, 1986).

PROMISING RETENTION STRATEGIES

In the evaluator's ideal world, each program would have used a different retention strategy to engage their families. Armed with this knowledge, we would have compared the relative success of each strategy and made some strong statements about effective methods for keeping disadvantaged families in family support services. In actuality, the nine programs used a variety of retention methods and had fairly similar attrition rates. However, the wealth of information from the parent interviews and the comparison of program completers to noncompleters suggested another approach to formulating a package of promising retention methods. To this end, we integrated the qualitative and quantitative findings along with a review of the relevant literature to propose some strategies we think have the potential to foster increased service participation among at-risk families.

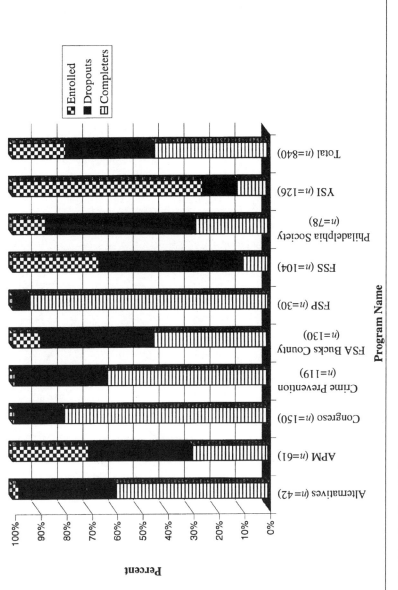

Figure 6.1. Participation Rates by Program

103

TABLE 6.1 Initial Differences Between Parents Completing Services and Parents Dropping Out

Significant Characteristics	Completers (n = 371)	Dropouts (n = 295)
Categorical Variables	Percentage	Percentage
Marital status***		
Never married	45.0	58.0
Ever married	50.4	38.6
Missing	4.6	3.4
Race, ethnicity***		
African American	41.8	58.6
Hispanic	35.0	17.6
White, non-Hispanic	21.3	20.3
Other	1.9	3.4
Public assistance***		
Yes	62.8	77.6
No	26.7	16.9
Missing	10.5	5.4
Employment*		
Employed	24.8	16.9
Not employed	75.2	83.1
Risk factors		
Difficulties with child care***	25.6	38.6
Children's placement**	12.9	6.6

Alleviating Economic Stress

One of the most consistent findings in the attrition literature is that families confronting large amounts of daily stress pose a higher risk of dropping out of voluntary services. For these parents, the demands of providing food, clothing, and shelter may leave little time or energy to seek out and actively use parenting programs (National Research Council, 1993). Indeed, for the Penn

TABLE 6.1 Continued

Significant Characteristics	Completers (n = 371)	Dropouts (n = 295)
Categorical Variables	*Percentage*	*Percentage*
Pregnancy, new baby†	22.4	29.2
Social isolation**	44.5	54.9
Adult functioning problems		
Inaccurate sense of child's needs**	66.0	77.4
Lack of child development knowledge	80.6	87.2
Excessive need for child to comply*	72.0	64.0
Low self-esteem*	66.6	75.3
Maltreatment potential		
Inadequate supervision**	16.4	27.1
Medical neglect*	9.2	15.9
Continuous Variables	*Mean (SD)*	*Mean (SD)*
Age***	29.4 (9.6)	26.7 (8.3)
Number of children*	2.4 (1.4)	2.6 (1.7)
Total risk factors*	2.8 (2.5)	3.2 (2.8)
Physical abuse potential (initial CAP scores)***	201 (99)	235 (105)

† $p < .08$
*$p < .05$; **$p < .01$; ***$p < .001$.

program participants, those who left services early encountered more financial stress than those who stayed. The primary demographic attributes separating noncompleters from program completers were poverty, youth, the absence of a partner, and larger family size. Even though these programs were able to engage at-risk families, a substantial number of those in the most disadvantaged circumstances did not choose to continue remaining actively involved through the parenting service.

These findings are not surprising; however, they clearly inform us that the service needs of an important group of parents are not being met. The combination of unemployment, receipt of public assistance, and the absence of a partner suggest a high level of economic stress for many families who drop out, confirming other studies noting that financially stressed mothers depart services at higher rates than mothers with more stable economic situations (Josten, Mullett, Savik, Campbell, & Vincent, 1995; Myers-Walls et al., 1997). In such circumstances, financial needs may take precedence over parenting issues. If this is true for many families, than rigid adherence to a specific parenting curriculum without recognition of more pressing needs may cause parents to withdraw from the program (Larner et al., 1992).

Program planners need to recognize the immediacy of economic concerns and either incorporate services designed to improve the financial conditions of families (e.g., adult literacy classes, GED programs) or link the family to such services in the community (e.g., WIC). In the current study, some program providers did help former participants obtain necessary services from other agencies. For example, staff from Philadelphia Society worked closely with participants to obtain housing, and YSI providers helped some of their participants start GED programs.

Research also indicates that stressed families are more responsive to services that include some form of concrete or material assistance (Barth et al., 1986; Fontana, Fleischman, McCarton, Meltzer, & Ruff, 1988). Such assistance can help to overcome certain logistical barriers, notably lack of child care or transportation, that dissuade parents from attending center-based services (Spoth et al., 1996). Though most of the Penn programs attempted to provide some type of logistical support to address these needs, we found that noncompleters had much greater difficulty securing child care than parents who completed services, suggesting that this barrier may have made the service inaccessible to many parents. Some center-based programs did provide child care services; however, we believe that the consistent inclusion of child care as an integral part of center-based services would help these and other family support programs retain more parents in service.

For parents who remained involved with the Penn programs, practical and concrete assistance, such as rides and Pampers, helped to sustain their continued participation. The following quote from an APM participant, mother of eight children (including two sets of twins) ranging in age from 6 months to 11 years old, explains the importance of practical assistance:

> It would be very difficult for me. I am currently receiving help, and without this help, it would be very difficult. Now, I have someone that takes me places and that does things for me. This is very important. This has always been very important to me, the women that come to my house.

We believe that such assistance functions as a reward and reinforcement for early program involvement. By providing families with a tangible example of the program's usefulness, especially in the initial months of service, the program can enlist families who may not perceive their parenting as in need of assistance.

Developmentally Appropriate Engagement Strategies

Adolescent mothers often prove hard to engage in either group (O'Leary et al., 1984) or home services (Josten et al., 1995), though one review reports that teen mothers were more likely to benefit from home-visiting programs (Olds & Kitzman, 1993). The current study found that younger parents, especially adolescents, were less likely to continue with services, as compared to older, more experienced mothers. As adolescent motherhood has been linked to a number of negative parenting behaviors and adverse outcomes for children (see Nath, Borkowski, Whitman, & Schellenbach, 1991), attracting young mothers to parenting programs is usually a top priority for program planners and policymakers.

The work of O'Leary et al. (1984) is instructive for methods to accomplish this feat. According to their perspective, the typical adolescent may avoid seeking help, as this conflicts with her need to establish independence. O'Leary and his colleagues recommend that program providers engage in persistent outreach with this group, recognizing that "no" from an adolescent may only reflect a need for greater or temporary distance from the provider rather than a desire for the termination of all help. The success of this approach is reflected in the following quote to a friend from an adolescent mother with two small children who attended the YSI program:

> I told her because she needed to get out and the kids was working on her nerves and I was like, Well come to the center and I'm going to give you the number and call them and talk to them. And once you'd come there, I said, "You'll be a little shy at the beginning, but sooner or later you'd get broken in, and they can help you. I can tell you what to do but I think it'd be best if you'd see."

Another origin of family stress that can affect program involvement is the movement from one stage of family development to another. For example, the experience of marriage, divorce, birth, or adoption usually calls for a transition period into a new developmental phase of family life where existing roles are adapted and assimilated to reflect the reformed family structure (Antonucci & Mikus, 1988). During this developmental period, conflict and tension often emerge, which disrupts the regular functioning of the parent and other family members. In the case of the Penn programs, the new phase exerting the most influence on program involvement was the experience of pregnancy or the presence of a new infant. Families encountering this type of change were more likely to drop out prematurely than families without a new infant.

This finding suggests that the multiple demands on a parent's physical and emotional health of caring for a new infant while struggling to make ends meet leave little excess energy for attending a parenting program. Because some experts posit that support programs achieve their greatest impact with new mothers (Larner et al., 1992), it is imperative that we find successful methods to recruit and engage such mothers in voluntary programs. Programs offering services in the home may prove more flexible for the parent and reduce some of the stress related to attending center-based services. In addition, the provision of services prenatally may create the necessary support and atmosphere of trust between the provider and parent that would facilitate the parent's ongoing program involvement after the child was born (Larson, 1980; Siegel et al., 1980; Weiss, 1993).

Culturally Relevant Services

In our earlier discussion of implementation barriers, we noted that cultural or community practices may operate against certain types of service modalities. Given the possibility of cultural specificity in program involvement, we were interested to observe that, regardless of the type of service received, racial heritage was connected to overall program retention. In our sample, African American mothers were more likely to leave services early, whereas Hispanics were more likely to complete services. Whites, on the other hand, were evenly split between those who completed the program and those who dropped out. Of course, we should note that the majority of Hispanics attended 10-week parent groups at Congreso, which may account for their higher completion rates. One would guess that finishing a 10-week workshop requires less commitment than a 6-month family intervention program. Still, these ethnic differences suggest a need for further research into the relationship between service attractiveness and cultural norms to determine if service delivery systems must be altered to appeal to various cultural groups (Pumariega, 1996).

Reducing Social Isolation

Merely offering an attractive service, however, will not ensure the involvement of families. As most program managers learn, parents often need assistance and encouragement to maintain their program involvement, especially in the case of isolated parents. It seems that such parents may not possess the skills to seek out help or to take advantage of assistance when it is offered (Crittenden, 1985; DePanfillis, 1996). For isolated families, attending center-based services or even allowing providers to see the family at home may seem overwhelming and beyond the parent's capability. When programs do succeed at engaging isolated parents, keeping them in service often becomes problematic. This proved the case in the current study where parents assessed as socially isolated at the time they entered services were more likely to drop out prematurely than parents who had access to a support network.

However, we were interested to learn that feelings of social isolation also predominated among the former participants, many of whom reported rarely leaving the house before becoming involved with the prevention programs. For them, the opportunity to get out of the house was a major enticement for service involvement. The following comments from a high-risk mother of four children, who participated in Philadelphia Society Services to Children's program, illustrates the perceived advantages of a support program, especially the importance of taking children out to play with other children and the chance to talk with other adults:

> I told them because they were young and with the kids you want to get out is the main thing. I told them you should go down there and sign up so you can get out some time and take the kids to be around different kids and play like that. I just told them to talk to the people because they babysit, anything, you are just drained. And, you come in and there is a lot to do. They keep you busy, and you get to spend more time with your children, and I notice that the things that they are doing that you may not see at home. There is a lot of things I told her. I can't remember everything. That was some of the main things.

Though social isolation may prevent a parent from enrolling in family support programs, the chance to alleviate both isolation and boredom also serves as an inducement for attending services. The dilemma for program developers is how to use this latter knowledge to engage parents in services. The work of the Penn programs and other research offers some guidance on this issue. For example, most programs made specific efforts to ensure participation in center-based activities by providing transportation and a meal to families. Furthermore, some programs used intensive home-based outreach both at the beginning of services and to follow up with families already engaged in services. Program managers reported that such efforts helped spur participant involvement. Our review of the social support literature suggests that programs might achieve more success with isolated parents if providers initially assess the parent's social skills (Fontana et al., 1988) and then focus on enhancing her interpersonal skills (Barth & Schinke, 1984; Beeman, 1995; DePanfillis, 1996). This process may give parents the tools necessary to feel successful in both group and home-based family support activities.

Identifying and Addressing Specific Parental Needs

Some work indicates that parents are more likely to remain in programs if they view the program as addressing an identified problem (Fontana et al., 1988; Larner et al., 1992; Olds & Kitzman, 1993). Whether stemming from the parent's perception that the child has a problem (e.g., not compliant or supportive enough) or the parent's acknowledgment of her own child-rearing limitations (e.g., overstressed), her expectation that the program can assist with the problem binds her to the service more completely than parents who do not perceive the program as meeting a specific need. Along these lines, we found that providers initially had rated program completers as significantly more likely to exhibit an excessive need for the child to comply with parental wishes. These parents may have viewed the service as a place that could help with their "problem" children, and this belief prompted parents to actively engage in services.

We also observed that parents who finished services were viewed as more likely to place inappropriate demands on their children for emotional support at the time of service initiation. Again, an unmet personal need appears to encourage parental involvement in family support services. Programs that stress enhancing child behavior through child management skill building may provide a nonthreatening atmosphere for overly demanding parents. An initial focus on changing child behavior removes the negative onus often associated with parenting programs, thereby encouraging participation.

We should note that a close to significant number of parents who stayed in the programs initially displayed an inability to manage anger and stress, suggesting that many high-risk parents engage in services because they recognize their own shortcomings and want to improve their children's lives. Of the follow-up parents, three quarters enrolled in the programs because they wanted help with their parenting skills. Although the majority tended to refer to seeking assistance with parenting in general, as indicated by responses such as they "wanted to be a better parent," others identified specific parenting concerns, such as understanding children's behavior (10%), discipline strategies (9%), communication skills (8%), and patience (7%). The ability of the provider to recognize and meet these needs not only encouraged participant involvement, it also accomplished the program's goal of improving parenting. For example, one provider helped a former Congreso participant understand what her 5-year-old was trying to say to her:

> Well, since I've gotten to know [staff], she talks to him. I would talk to him and he would sit down and if he would tell me something, I would try to see what it means. He tells me this and this. And she would tell me, she would give me an explanation for it all. I would go home and I would talk to him again on it and then he would tell me the same thing and I would understand what he meant then.

This quote highlights two critical mechanisms for meeting the needs of these parents: showing the parent how to be empathetic with the child and fostering the parent's ability to truly understand her child's words and actions. With increased empathy, understanding, and patience, a parent also becomes less likely to experience frustration and anger when confronting challenging child behavior.

For a small percentage of families, involvement in these programs may have been spurred by a more urgent need: the desire to be reunited with a child. Though only 10% of parents had children in placement, defined as children living in foster care or under Child Protective Services supervision, these parents were more likely to complete a service cycle. This finding may simply indicate, however, that parents with children in placement are required to complete a prevention service if they wish to regain custody of their children.

The Parent-Provider Relationship

Perhaps the key ingredient to successfully retaining disadvantaged families in support services is the development of a trusting, dependable connection between the parent and provider. Studies examining the parent-provider relationship have found a number of factors thought to enhance participation, such as mutual agreement of the presenting problem (Epperson, Bushway, & Warman, 1983; Tyron & Tyron, 1986), clear communication (Tyron & Tyron, 1986), and the inclusion of the participant in setting up the first visit (Josten, Reckinger, Frederickson, Savik, & Cross, 1997). In the current study, parental interviews revealed two additional facets of this relationship that fostered program involvement: the perception of the provider as a friend (Powell, 1990) and the ability of the provider to establish some level of trust during the initial program contacts. For example, former participants remembered their staff person as someone they could depend on and confide in and who never made them feel like "bad parents." In fact, one YSI participant described her family care worker as a "true friend." When the interviewer asked how she knew that, she replied, "Because she was there for me no matter what, no sleep, I don't care what kind of weather it was, where she was at. If she could make it, she was here." Furthermore, this participant attributed her motivation to improve her life to her family care worker. Thus, establishing a foundation of trust with the family through persistence, reliability, and nonjudgmental dialogue encourages parents to remain with the service, especially if accomplished during the preliminary stages of program involvement.

The use of positive reinforcement techniques also helps build a strong connection to the provider. Low self-esteem and feelings of inadequacy can overwhelm a parent, tempting her to give up efforts to improve her situation. Training and supervision of providers around methods for enhancing parental self-worth and increasing feelings of self-efficacy can prevent this from occurring. The following quote from a mother of four children, also entrusted with the care of an infant grandson, vividly demonstrates the success of such techniques:

> Sometimes, I sell myself out, like I make myself the blame for a lot of things that's happening in my life. And then I tell [Crime Prevention staff] and she talks about different things, why is it not my fault and talks to me about why you are putting yourself down when you are not that type of person. She builds my self-esteem back up.

CRITICAL INDICATORS OF FUTURE NONINVOLVEMENT

As we have seen, completers differed from dropouts in several ways. To determine which of these characteristics were the most important predictors of leaving services early, we employed forward logistical regression analysis (see Resource B). This method selects the most significant variables, in order of importance, and enters them one at a time into the regression equation. Variables that do not significantly contribute to the model are omitted from the regression equation. With this method, we determined which of the significant demographic characteristics, risk factors, adult functioning problems, and maltreatment indicators described earlier best explained whether a parent completed or dropped out of services. In these analyses, we excluded the 10% of families with children in placement, as such families either had previous child maltreatment reports or were mandated to attend parenting services and therefore could not be considered voluntary participants.

The results indicated that the odds of dropping out from these voluntary prevention programs significantly increased for parents who received public assistance, were of young maternal age, and were of non-Hispanic origin. Maltreatment indicators also played a role, as initially high CAP scores and a potential for inadequate supervision increased the likelihood that a parent would prematurely exit from the prevention program. It is interesting that none of the risk factors or adult functioning problems contributed statistically to determining drop-out status. We need to remember, however, that the presence of any of these factors, either alone or in combination, cannot accurately predict who will engage and who will not. Still, program staff should be aware that families with this constellation of characteristics may prove more challenging to retain in services and may require extra efforts and attention.

LESSONS LEARNED

The task confronting these nine programs and, indeed, all voluntary family support programs, is creating and sustaining a mutually satisfying match between the family's needs and what the program has to offer. That task becomes even more formidable when programs work with the types of overburdened families attracted through the Penn Initiative. These results indicate that many specific characteristics associated with an elevated risk for parenting difficulties are more prevalent among parents who drop out of services. Though the findings described earlier primarily reflect the experience of these Philadelphia programs and may not translate beyond this group, we believe that awareness of these key markers can advance efforts to structure effective engagement and retention strategies.

Service Providers

- Providers may need to exert extra efforts to retain young mothers in services, especially those who receive public assistance. Some of the tactics noted earlier, such as offering a variety of material incentives, helping the mother finish school, and engaging in aggressive outreach and follow-up, should become strategies routinely used with this population.

- We have recommended that programs attempt to address the personal needs of the parents in addition to parenting concerns (Weiss, 1993). Potentially, however, this approach could foster dependency if the programs attempt do everything for the mother. Managers must closely monitor the service delivery process to ensure that providers create an appropriate balance between supporting the parent and conveying the key parenting and child-rearing concepts that are the heart of the program.

- The critical impact of the parent-provider relationship underscores the need for program management to provide the supports necessary for providers to establish these connections with families. Adequate training and supervision, along with reasonable caseloads, are necessary to foster provider competence.

- The high attrition rates found in this and other studies should prompt some hard questions about the program's service model. We think that including potential participants in the service design phase would help avoid some of this attrition. Once service delivery has begun, managers then need to track retention rates and investigate possible reasons why families are dropping out at rates higher than expected. Assessing the fidelity of the actual service delivery process to the program model should be the first step in this process.

Funders and Policymakers

- Though often not considered an integral part of support services, the provision of child care, transportation, and other material and logistical supports to parents appears to be a key component of successful retention strategies. Funders should consider such activities a critical ingredient of the service design and support grant allocations addressing these areas.

- As noted throughout this book, our empirical knowledge base currently has little to offer concerning why families choose to participate or to avoid voluntary support services, despite the importance of such information for program success. We advocate that more research dollars be allocated to investigate engagement and retention in voluntary programs to redress these shortcomings.

- From both a policy and planning perspective, these findings suggest that programs encounter some families for whom voluntary family support services are simply inadequate. Enrolling and retaining in programs parents who display a high potential for abuse or neglect yet have little interest or motivation for engaging in parenting services may be an impossible task for voluntary programs (Larner et al., 1992; Daro, 1988). It is quite likely that many resistant families will only enroll in parenting programs if required to do so. Furthermore, such parents may require the type of intensive, therapeutic counseling services not typically provided by family support programs. Recognizing the broad spectrum of families referred to such programs, our experience suggests that providers and planners must come to terms with the knowledge that not all parents can be adequately served through family support efforts.

Researchers

- More work needs to investigate why many disadvantaged families agree to enroll but fail to follow through with voluntary services. Does the program not live up to their expectations, or do daily life stressors and crises prevent them from taking advantage of this opportunity? As noted earlier, research needs to pay more attention to engagement issues and needs to incorporate both qualitative and quantitative methods when examining these concerns.

NOTE

1. The follow-up sample differs from this larger sample in two ways. First, the follow-up sample represents parents at the higher end of the risk continuum. Members of the follow-up sample tended to have more children, to be single, to have lower incomes, and to be Hispanic or African American than was true for the total evaluation sample. We also found these same demographic characteristics, with the exception of Hispanic heritage, to be strongly associated with leaving the prevention programs prematurely. Second, over half (56%) of the follow-up sample joined the prevention programs either through their own volition or at the encouragement of a friend, unlike the full sample, where the majority heard about the programs from a professional source, such as a social worker or nurse.

CHAPTER 7

Future Directions

SUMMARY

Over 10 years have elapsed since the Penn Foundation first placed its resources into the Child Abuse Prevention Initiative. During this decade, we have witnessed remarkable changes in the child welfare system, though it remains to be seen whether these changes will ultimately enrich or diminish the lives of children. On the plus side, most players in the family support field, from policymakers, to funders, to providers and social scientists, have reached a consensus that society must find ways to prevent family breakdown and dysfunction, rather than waiting to fix the family after it is broken. The latest buzzwords, "early intervention," reflect this new direction, as more and more programs target families with young children to help forge a strong, nurturing bond between parent and child right from the start, with the hope that such support will prevent child maltreatment, school failure, violence, and other troublesome behaviors all too prevalent in today's families. Early Head Start, Healthy Families America, Parents as Teachers, and Home Visitation 2000 are among the numerous efforts that have sprung up in the past decade or so to meet the needs of young families. Increasingly, hospitals, schools, and community agencies across the United States offer some form of parenting support, especially to first-time parents. Collectively, these efforts represent a considerable commitment to both prevention and to families.

On the minus side, the number of children physically or mentally harmed continues to climb. For example, the most recent national incidence figures indicate that serious injuries to children by their caregivers quadrupled in just 7 years (Sedlak & Broadhurst, 1996). Despite the staggering increase in maltreatment, Child Protective Services persists in serving roughly the same number of families as in past years (Sedlak & Broadhurst, 1996; U.S. Department of Health and Human Services, 1998; Wang & Daro, 1998). This has prompted some observers to state that CPS has reached its capacity because families who are at the breaking point may no longer have access to support services that were available in previous years (Daro & McCurdy, 1994; Schorr, 1997; Sedlak & Broadhurst, 1996). The elimination of welfare, as we have known it, represents another contraction in the safety net of family services. Destitute families can no longer rely on government programs to help feed, clothe, or shelter their children. Although some argue that such assistance only caused more problems for the parent, most are wondering what will happen to the children of those parents who cannot or will not support themselves.

As public priorities change and government funding opportunities diminish, the triumphs and failures of the Penn Initiative have extended our understanding of how to successfully support families in struggling communities. The story told here captures the conflict between the familial desire to better children's lives and the obstacles that can block this aspiration and sheds some light on the varied avenues that lead to success. In this chapter, we highlight the most valuable insights we derived from this Initiative and also ponder some of the unanswered questions that remain. Because the experiences of these nine parenting programs reflect the types of intervention strategies commonly employed by family support programs, the lessons learned from the Penn Initiative contain important implications for many of the prevention efforts underway across the country.

MAJOR INSIGHTS

Perhaps our most significant discovery was the magnitude of interest in voluntary parenting services among families residing in disadvantaged communities, such as those in Philadelphia. Despite often horrendous living conditions and bleak histories of childhood deprivation that included abuse and neglect for many, most of these high-risk parents wished to give their children the best parenting possible. Like parents in more stable communities have done for years, these families took advantage of voluntary, neighborhood-based programs once they were available, proving that the urge to do everything possible for one's children cuts across all income lines. Not all families were helped by the programs, and one third elected to drop out early; but the fact that over 1,000 families even took the time to enroll clearly signals a tremendous, heretofore unmet demand for parenting services and information. Other community-based, privately funded initiatives have noted a similar demand for services among vulnerable families (Larner et al., 1992; Owen & Fercello, 1998), suggesting that this may be a widespread need. Our challenge is to meet this need with quality services that respect and value families.

How to institute and maintain a quality service that appeals to high-risk families is the $60 million question for the family support field. Although in need of further verification through future studies, some key program elements emerged from this research that should prove helpful to those seeking to create effective interventions. Employing aggressive, community-based outreach to families (e.g., door-to-door canvassing) to promote services; building in mechanisms to reduce participant attrition, such as transportation assistance, food, child care, and respite services (Barth et al., 1986); closely matching the service to the family's needs (Schorr, 1997); and providing adequate support for parents both in setting realistic goals for changing their discipline approaches and in working to overcome barriers to these goals are a few of the ingredients that seem to attract high-risk families and to assist them in becoming better parents.

What we believe to be a core element of a successful family support program, however, relates to a factor often associated with improved parenting: intensity of services. Our follow-up analyses and other studies (see Guterman, 1997; Powell & Grantham-McGregor, 1989; Schorr, 1988) have reported that more intensive services correspond to better outcomes. But what does this finding really mean? The lesson applied by many observers is that services must be frequent (i.e., at least weekly), of sufficient duration (i.e., lasting 6 months or more), and accessible to the family (Guterman, 1997; Thompson, 1995) to qualify as intensive. Although these program elements are important, our conclusion is somewhat different. We believe that the findings around intensity more likely reflect a flourishing relationship between the provider and participant. That is, families who like, respect, and believe they can learn from their provider will be more likely to fully participate in and benefit from the program than those who do not hold these opinions. For some providers, this connection may be established with less than weekly contact; for others, even intensive services will not guarantee success. In our parent interviews, many mothers revealed that the personal connection with the provider was what kept them involved in services. In fact, most participants equated the program with the staff.

As noted by Lisbeth Schorr (1997), "Staff in successful programs take on an extended role in the lives of the children and families they work with" (p. 6). Our interview data confirm this belief, as most long-term participants gave us detailed accounts of staff "going the extra mile" for them. Of course, translating this knowledge about valuable provider qualities into a practical program element presents a challenge. We agree with our participants and other observers (Daro, 1998; Schorr, 1997; Slaughter-Defoe, 1993) that the primary attributes of an outstanding provider are compassion, sensitivity, a nonjudgmental attitude, and respect for and an understanding of the family's life circumstances. Adequate training, supervision, clear program goals, and manageable caseloads must also be present for providers to maintain these sought-after qualities. Programs that seek out these characteristics in their staff and offer this supportive work environment will stand out as exemplary family support programs.

Unfortunately, establishing a trusting, mutually respectful parent-provider relationship may not be enough to help some parents substantially alter their child-rearing practices. Our parent interviews showed that many mothers found it too exhausting and difficult to battle against the parenting norms of friends and family by adhering to new child-rearing strategies that had been learned in the programs. A sizable portion were criticized as too lenient, told that their children were in need of some physical discipline to avoid being spoiled or needed to learn about respect. This criticism wore down some mothers, who reverted to their previous discipline habits, whereas others chose to incorporate the parenting program's methods into their more aggressive parenting styles. Consequently, one core element for success involves program planners and staff helping parents persevere in the face of vocal resistance to new parenting strategies.

In addition, we found some behavior, seemingly at odds with more middle-class parenting ideas, arising from very functional and realistic circumstances, such as the need to keep children safe. In this study, the threat of neighborhood violence often operated against significant, long-term parenting gains. For some mothers, the need to restrict their children's activities and to expect immediate compliance to protect them from harm overrode all else. Such parents found it hard to encourage exploratory behavior or to refrain from yelling or hitting when the child appeared to disobey or ignore parental requests.

Last, close ties between the provider and parent did not always lead to improved child-rearing attitudes. For some of the more isolated mothers, the provider became a primary support source, helping to reduce loneliness and depression. Unfortunately, this aid did not transform the mother into a more nurturing caregiver, even though her personal outlook had improved. Another group of parents appeared more interested in meeting their own needs than those of their children. For these mothers, program involvement offered an opportunity to leave the house, to socialize with other adults, or to have someone else watch their children, as opposed to a chance to create a healthier home environment.

Because of these issues, we have come to regard a close provider-parent relationship as a necessary but insufficient condition for success, if one defines success as sustained improvements in parenting. Proponents of the ecological approach have long argued for programmatic models that take into account the myriad influences on families (Bronfenbrenner, 1979; Cicchetti & Lynch, 1993; Vondra & Belsky, 1993). The results from the Penn Initiative vividly illustrate that by ignoring these broader influences, family support programs may only achieve limited, short-term gains in parental attitudes and behavior among families residing in unstable, chaotic communities. Although helping such individuals to broaden their parenting knowledge and skills is a worthy undertaking, as even short-term enhancements in the child-rearing environment may lead to some long-term benefits for a child (Perry, 1995; Perry, Pollard, Blakley, Baker, & Vigilante, 1995), if we fail to acknowledge and address that parenting occurs within a family system and that the family system itself is profoundly shaped by community forces (Schorr, 1997), these gains most likely will erode over time.

Successful programs, then, must base their philosophy and program objectives on ecological models that address internal and external influences on parenting. In the case of the Penn Initiative, many programs incorporated aspects of an ecological approach, such as attempting to link the family to other community resources and offering support groups to expand parent networks. However, the principal program focus rested more narrowly on the parent-child dyad. Typically, provider efforts were directed at ameliorating internal barriers to parenting, such as insufficient parenting knowledge or unrealistic expectations for the child. Most program managers and providers failed to consider the powerful influence on parenting behavior exerted by external forces, such as other family members and the community at large, until these forces came into conflict with program goals.

We advocate widening the principal program focus to capture other integral forces affecting the family. Although these forces range from parental work conditions (Belsky, 1984) to poverty (Halpern, 1993; McLoyd, 1990) and racism (NCPCA, 1996), we concentrate our recommendations on those areas most easily influenced by a family support program. As a first step, providers need to identify the primary parental support network, such as grandparents or significant others. Once identified, an in-depth understanding must emerge around these key figures as to their positive and negative influence on the mother and her child-rearing style. If possible, these figures should be recruited into services along with the mother to create a broader foundation of support for new parenting methods.

The next critical step involves determining how and why current child-rearing patterns evolved and to what degree external forces, such as cultural and communal beliefs regarding appropriate and necessary methods to ensure child safety, support the status quo. Equipped with this knowledge, providers can begin to construct effective service plans that take into account the family and community systems that affect child rearing. At a minimum, such an approach requires extensive staff training on cultural issues and methods to build rapport and assess familial relationships and parental motivation for joining the service. Such training must also include instructions on how to engage participants in open discussions about potential or actual conflict between program goals and norms with family and community norms. To address broader influences on parenting, program managers will need to forge partnerships with community entities that influence child-rearing patterns, such as religious groups, respected community leaders, neighborhood associations, and educational institutions.

UNANSWERED QUESTIONS

In a study of this nature, the results often create more questions than answers. Although our efforts have largely gone toward drawing the most important lessons learned from the Initiative, we think it is equally valuable to explore some of the more critical questions that arose during the course of our investigation. Two issues grabbed our attention as requiring further contemplation by all audiences targeted in this book—policymakers, providers, researchers, and funders. The first, how to define and measure success, is a longstanding concern but has gained in importance as funders and policymakers require programs to prove their worth. The second issue, attrition, is the Achilles' heel of many, if not most, voluntary family support programs. Too often, families agree to participate only to disappear a few weeks or months into the service cycle. Although these two issues are no doubt related, we discuss each as a separate concern.

In working with high-risk families, we have begun to wonder how one can best define and measure success. As social scientists, we typically base our definition on the program's stated goals and then choose measures that we hope accurately assess these goals. Our interviews with parents, however, have caused us to think about success from their viewpoint. Many parents joined these programs with specific aims—to be a better parent than their own parent(s), to find ways to avoid yelling at or hitting their child, or to provide a more nurturing home than their friends and neighbors. By program and evaluation standards, a number of high-risk parents failed to improve their parenting over time. By parental standards, however, success had occurred. They hit or yelled at their children less; they talked to and reasoned with their children more; they provided a healthier environment in comparison to their friends or family. Should these parents be considered failures and the program ineffective? Whose standard of success is more important, the program's or the parent's? Do policymakers, planners, funders, and researchers help create a cycle of failure by holding unrealistic expectations for vulnerable parents (Halpern, 1993)? Although we cannot provide any clear answers to this dilemma, we would like to see more discussion on these issues in the family support field.

In this book, we saw that vulnerable families appear to benefit from family support efforts and that those at highest risk can improve their parental attitudes through voluntary service participation. We must note, however, that the Penn programs experienced a sizable amount of attrition over the course of services, with 35% failing to complete the full service cycle. Even though high attrition rates are a common occurrence in voluntary support programs (see McCurdy, Hurvis, & Clark, 1996), a more troubling aspect concerns which families dropped out. In this study, the more dysfunctional families were the ones that terminated services early. Parents who dropped out had elevated scores both on the initial CAP and on ratings of potential to engage in inadequate supervision and medical neglect, and they also evidenced a greater propensity to be single parents and to receive public assistance than those who stayed. Thus, although the Penn programs were able to serve many families often considered too problematic for family support efforts, there remained a substantial group of the highest-risk families who failed to take complete advantage of the voluntary services, even after expending the energy to enroll in services.

That leaves us with the question of what to do with extremely high-risk parents. Should they be mandated into services even though they have yet to harm a child, a practice that would swamp an already overburdened child welfare system? Or have we not been able to devise a system of support that appeals to such families? Although it is heartening that so many disadvantaged families made an attempt to access parenting services, the fact that one third decided to leave prematurely reflects a failure to construct a service that genuinely meets their needs. We believe that planners and researchers should direct greater efforts toward understanding vulnerable families' needs before policymakers turn to more punitive approaches. Too often, as professionals, we assume that parents are unaware or unwilling to talk about what they need to become better parents. Interviews with former participants, however, illustrate that parents who are struggling can be quite articulate in describing their needs and appreciate the opportunity to voice an opinion. Before program implementation, planners would be well-advised to conduct needs assessments or focus groups with potential consumers to ensure that the planned service is attractive to the target population. In fact, this dialogue should be an ongoing facet of services, therefore making the program-parent relationship a collaborative alliance (Schorr, 1997), rather than the more top-down, authoritarian structure that currently exists in most support programs.

From a research perspective, more studies need to investigate factors related to engagement and retention (McCurdy et al., 1996). Increasing knowledge about why parents elect to stay in services as well as why many choose to drop out would help us understand if barriers to service involvement can be addressed through programmatic modifications or not. Comparing the service delivery process of programs with high retention rates to those with more limited success may also shed some light on how to create effective interventions.

FUTURE DIRECTIONS

What will be the legacy of the William Penn Foundation's Child Abuse Prevention Initiative? Should this partnership between a foundation and a number of private, nonprofit organizations serve as a model for future initiatives? In our experience, several features of this collaboration exemplify some "best" standards that most prevention efforts should include. The decision to allow community agencies to design a service package reflecting their constituents' needs, the investment by a private entity in child welfare, the continued fiscal support of programs past the pilot stage, the requirement that each program participate in both process and outcome evaluations, and the decision to target support services to families living in disadvantaged neighborhoods represent some of the critical components that contributed not only to the Initiative's success but also to its relevance to current and future family support endeavors.

Given the new knowledge generated by this study, we would also recommend some changes to this family support model. First of all, we believe that programs need to be fiscally supported for a minimum of 5 years, with the expectation that program start-up will absorb at least the first year of operations. The 3-year grant periods common to the field means that programs just achieve stability only to become consumed by the quest for more resources, with adverse effects on service delivery. Second, requiring programs to participate in an evaluation does not guarantee that evaluation findings inform the program's future development. To address this weakness, we propose that funding sources require evaluators and program managers to establish feedback mechanisms that allow important data and findings to guide refinement of the service delivery process and that ensure that such information is easily accessed and understood by program staff.

Third, the use of private dollars to fund prevention efforts signals a considerable investment in a community; however, few foundations or other private funding sources can supply the necessary infrastructure and long-term assistance needed to establish a sustainable family support program. Frequently, a termination in private funding means a termination of services. We believe sustainable programs are more likely to emerge through partnerships between private funders and publicly funded entities, such as a local department of health or social services or statewide Children's Trust Funds. Private funders can help facilitate partnerships by requiring programs to seek matching grants or by teaming up with the public sector during the initial planning stages. With the combined energies of both public and private sectors invested in family support efforts, we may be able to build communities that strengthen families.

This brings us to our final point—the need to direct efforts toward building what the 1990 U.S. Advisory Board on Child Abuse and Neglect called "caring communities" (U.S. Advisory Board on Child Abuse and Neglect, 1991). In our estimation, individual approaches to family support, that is, working with one family at a time, will not stem the tide of family deterioration. Although that one family can access needed resources and help, others cannot and may then experience further disintegration. Many families live in communities with excessive violence, no parks or play areas, dangerous housing stock, and streets filled with people engaged in illegal enterprises. If the community itself endangers the child, how can such families provide safe and caring homes (Garbarino &

Sherman, 1980)? Other families live in safe, clean neighborhoods with all the amenities; yet some children go unsupervised while parents and neighbors ignore signs of trouble. Until concerted efforts are made to create healthy, child-friendly communities, those involved in family support can expect to achieve only limited success in lowering child maltreatment rates, increasing child safety, and helping children achieve their full potential. Others have detailed some of the steps needed to realize these goals (Schorr, 1997; Thompson, 1995); some public and private agencies have begun targeting resources in this direction with varying degrees of impact. From our vantage point, family support and prevention advocates must join together and champion community-wide support efforts.

Resource A:
Methodology

The nine programs articulated a range of prevention goals for the participants, such as enhanced parent-child interaction, increased cognitive development of the child, and greater social support for the family, yet all shared a common theme: to prevent child maltreatment. In choosing outcome measures that would both capture the individual program's intent yet not place considerable data burdens on the program staff, we elected to focus on this common theme of child abuse prevention.

CHILD ABUSE POTENTIAL INVENTORY (CAP)

As discussed in Chapter 1, we selected as our dependent variable a self-report measure of potential for physical abuse, the Child Abuse Potential Inventory (CAP; Milner, 1986). The CAP measures parental potential for physical maltreatment and consists of 160 items with which the respondent agrees or disagrees. The CAP contains six subscales assessing qualities related to physical abuse potential: rigidity, distress, loneliness, problems with self and child, problems with family, and problems with others. The CAP has been subjected to extensive validity and reliability testing (see Milner, 1986). In this sample, CAP scores ranged from 0 to 455. Higher scores correspond to a greater potential for physical abuse. Parents completed the CAP within 2 weeks of program entry and again at program termination. In accordance with established practice, we excluded the scores of participants with 10% or more missing data on the CAP. Out of the original 840 participants, 490 had usable CAPs at entry to and termination from services.

To measure improvements in parenting, we assessed the impact of the nine programs on final CAP scores. The initial program differences described in Chapter 3 were controlled through the use of multivariate analyses. We selected the following variables as our control variables: (a) initial CAP scores to adjust for the varying levels of risk across programs in potential for physical abuse; (b) the five demographic variables that significantly varied across the programs (maternal age, number of children, marital status [never vs. ever married]), educational attainment (no high school degree vs. high school graduate), and income (under $15,000 vs. over); (c) cohort to account for differences between the subjects participating in the first study between 1990 and 1992 (Cohort 1) and those who participated in the second round of data collection between 1993 and 1995 (Cohort 2); (d) referral source, to adjust for programmatic differences in recruitment between informal referrals (self-initiated or by peers), formal (social worker or other professional), and other source (e.g., religious personnel); and (e) service intensity, defined as number of weekly program contacts.

Although participant race significantly varied across programs, this variable was not selected as a control due to its high correlation ($r = .8$) with program. As noted earlier, programs tended to serve participants of one racial or ethnic background. Alternatives, the suburban program, was the only site with a racially mixed sample. This confound between race and program meant that we could not have both variables in the same regression equation. Instead, we first assessed the impact of all programs without controlling for race or ethnicity. We then analyzed program impact among programs serving similar ethnic populations.

To ensure a conservative test of program effects, we chose a hierarchical regression model. On the first step, we entered initial CAP scores into the regression equation. The next step included the five demographic variables, cohort, and referral source. The third step entered all of the programs, with Congreso as the minimal service comparison program. Last, we entered the service characteristics. We then analyzed whether the input of programs into the equation produced a significant change in the explained variance (R^2 change) and if participation at an individual program produced a significant impact on final CAP scores. We substituted the mean score for any missing data.

LIKELIHOOD TO ENGAGE IN
MALTREATING BEHAVIORS

We asked staff to make clinical judgments regarding parental likelihood to engage in several types of maltreatment. At intake and termination, parents were rated on a four-point Likert scale ranging from 1 (*very likely*) to 4 (*very unlikely*) to engage in the following seven behaviors: excessive use of corporal punishment; inadequate child supervision; emotional neglect; physical, medical, and educational neglect; and failure to protect the child from abuse from others. Staff initially rated over 86% as unlikely to engage in physical, medical, or educational neglect or failure to protect the child. Consequently, we limited our analyses to changes in corporal punishment, inadequate supervision, and emotional neglect.

We employed two analytic techniques to study change in maltreatment likelihood. First, we conducted paired *t* tests to assess whether a significant change in participant scores occurred at each site. Thus, paired *t* tests provided us with a picture of within-program change. To assess across-program effects, we created an ordinal-level, dependent outcome with three categories: increased likelihood for maltreatment between entry and termination, no change, and decreased likelihood for maltreatment over the course of services. Because this outcome variable has an ordinal level of measurement, we selected a nonparametric test, the Kruskal-Wallis (Downing & Clark, 1997), to compare the distribution of these dependent variables across the nine programs. The Kruskal-Wallis test of independent samples is similar to a one-way ANOVA. It tests for significant differences in the distribution of a variable between two or more independent groups. It rank orders the data and uses a chi-square statistic to test the null hypothesis that all programs produce a similar effect.

Our inability to subject this outcome measure to multivariate statistical analyses prevented us from taking into account the obvious program differences in the initial risk level of the parents before examining the impact of the nine programs. For example, participants at Alternatives and Crime Prevention had a greater likelihood of improving because staff initially judged them at a high level of risk. In addition, the amount of change in maltreating behaviors noted by staff may be more reflective of staff or program characteristics than actual change on the part of the parents. For example, programs using counseling or detailed parent interviews may be more likely to observe change in parenting practices than programs with less intensive interactions with the parent (e.g., large group workshops). Overall, findings regarding CAP are more robust than those concerning staff assessments of parental likelihood to engage in maltreating behaviors.

LIKELIHOOD TO DROP OUT OF SERVICES

In assessing the likelihood that a parent would exit services prematurely, we first made bivariate comparisons between parents completing services ($n = 371$) and those dropping out prior to the end of services ($n = 295$). We excluded parents from these analyses who were still receiving services at the time the study ended. Significant differences between completers and dropouts are presented in Table 6.1. As discussed in Chapter 6, we then used stepwise logistic regression analyses to isolate the most significant predictors of dropping out. The dichotomous dependent variable, dropped out early, is coded as 1= yes and 0 = no. All the independent variables listed in Table 6.1 were included in this analysis. As described in Chapter 6, the stepwise method enters the dependent variables in order of significance until all significant variables are in the equation. This method excludes variables that significantly distinguish completers from dropouts in the bivariate analyses if they lose their significance when other factors are included in the equation. Subjects with any missing data were excluded from these analyses ($n = 128$).

Resource B:
Data Analyses

TABLE B.1 Hierarchical Regression Analyses Predicting Final CAP Scores for All Participants

Independent Variables (omitted category)	Beta Coeffecient	t Value	R^2 Change
Initial CAP Score	.66	18.3	0.44***
Demographic characteristics			0.02**
Maternal age	.06	1.3	
Number of children	−.02	−0.6	
Never married (vs. ever married)	.07	1.5	
No high school (vs. graduate)	.02	0.4	
Low income (vs. $15,000 plus)	.05	1.2	
Cohort 1 (vs. Cohort 2)	−.02	−0.5	
Informal referral (vs. formal)	−.10	−2.5**	
Other referral source (vs. formal)	−.03	−0.8	
Program (vs. Congreso)			.01****
Alternatives	.01	0.3	
APM	−.04	−0.9	
Crime Prevention	.01	0.2	
FSA of Bucks County	−.11	−2.3*	

TABLE B.1 Continued

Independent Variables (omitted category)	Beta Coeffecient	t Value	R^2 Change
FSP	–.01	–0.4	
FSS	.03	0.8	
Philadelphia Society	–.04	–0.08	
YSI	.04	0.8	
Service intensity			.00
Weekly program contacts	.01	0.1	

NOTE: $N = 490$; final equation adjusted $R^2 = .46$; $F = 25.7$ (df 17); $p < .0001$.
$*p < .05; **p < .01; ***p < .001$.

TABLE B.2 Change in Likelihood to Engage in Excessive Use of Corporal Punishment: Analysis of All Participants

Program	t *Tests* Mean Change in Scores		Kruskal-Wallis	
	Mean	*(SD)*	*Mean Rank*	*(Rank Order)*
Alternatives (*n* = 34)	.21	(1.1)	345.01	(5)
APM (*n* = 47)	.47	(0.9)***	395.26	(1)
Congreso (*n* = 125)	.34	(0.7)***	362.58	(3)
Crime Prevention (*n* = 87)	.37	(0.8)***	365.14	(2)
FSA of Bucks County (*n* = 119)	.25	(0.6)***	339.59	(6)
FSP (*n* = 25)	−.12	(0.8)	259.34	(9)
FSS (*n* = 74)	.31	(0.7)***	349.46	(4)
Philadelphia Society (*n* = 59)	.02	(0.6)*	332.47	(7)
YSI (*n* = 111)	.05	(0.9)	292.37	(8)
			Chi-Square	
All programs (*n* = 681)	.25	(0.8)***	22.83**	

$*p < .05; **p < .01; ***p < .001.$

TABLE B.3 Change in Likelihood to Engage in Inadequate Supervision: Analysis of
All Participants

	t *Tests* Mean Change in Scores		Kruskal-Wallis	
Program	*Mean*	*(SD)*	*Mean Rank*	*(Rank Order)*
Alternatives (*n* = 34)	−.03	(1.9)	321.32	(6)
APM (*n* = 47)	.34	(0.7)**	384.70	(1)
Congreso (*n* = 125)	.24	(1.1)**	372.41	(2)
Crime Prevention (*n* = 87)	.29	(0.8)**	362.99	(3)
FSA of Bucks County (*n* = 119)	.15	(0.7)*	339.78	(4)
FSP (*n* = 25)	−.12	(0.5)	281.98	(9)
FSS (*n* = 74)	.00	(0.8)	302.63	(8)
Philadelphia Society (*n* = 59)	.02	(0.7)	312.8	(7)
YSI (*n* = 111)	.10	(1.1)	331.09	(5)
			Chi-Square	
All programs (*n* = 681)	.14	(0.9)***	17.84*	

$*p < .05; **p < .01; ***p < .001.$

TABLE B.4 Change in Likelihood to Be Emotionally Uninvolved: Analysis of All
Participants

	t *Tests* Mean Change in Scores		*Kruskal-Wallis*	
Program	*Mean*	*(SD)*	*Mean Rank*	*(Rank Order)*
Alternatives (*n* = 34)	.44	(1.0)**	389.44	(2)
APM (*n* = 47)	.36	(0.6)***	367.84	(3)
Congreso (*n* = 125)	.30	(1.0)***	360.34	(4)
Crime Prevention (*n* = 87)	.52	(0.9)***	398.76	(1)
FSA of Bucks County (*n* = 119)	.23	(0.8)**	335.06	(5)
FSP (*n* = 25)	−.04	(0.5)	275.96	(9)
FSS (*n* = 74)	.16	(1.0)	326.18	(6)
Philadelphia Society (*n* = 59)	.12	(0.6)†	309.14	(7)
YSI (*n* = 111)	.02	(1.1)	295.59	(8)
			Chi-Square	
All programs (*N* = 681)	.25	(0.9)***	28.4***	

†$p < .08$; **$p < .01$; ***$p < .001$.

TABLE B.5   Hierarchical Regression Analyses Predicting Final CAP Scores for
High-Risk Participants[a]

Independent Variables (omitted category)	Beta Coeffecient	t Value	R^2 Change
Initial CAP Score	.38	5.6***	.13***
Demographic characteristics			.06†
Maternal age	.14	1.9†	
Number of children	.01	0.1	
Never married (vs. ever married)	.20	2.5*	
No high school (vs. graduate)	−.06	−0.7	
Low income (vs. $15,000 plus)	−.02	−0.3	
Cohort 1 (vs. Cohort 2)	.00	0	
Informal referral (vs. formal)	−.12	−1.7	
Other referral source (vs. formal)	−.01	−0.1	
Program[b] (vs. Congreso)			.07**
APM	−.14	−1.5	
Crime Prevention	−.06	−0.7	
FSA of Bucks County	−.24	−2.5**	
FSS	−.02	−0.2	
Philadelphia Society	−.20	−2.4*	
YSI	.04	0.4	
Service intensity			.01
Weekly contacts	.10	1.3	

NOTE: $N = 217$; final equation adjusted, $R^2 = .20$; $F = 4.35$ (df 16); $p < .0001$.
a. Participants scoring 215 or more on the initial CAP.
b. These analyses excluded participants from Alternatives and FSP due to small sample size ($n < 10$ at each).
†$p = < .06$; **$p < .01$; ***$p < .001$; ****$p < .0001$; $n < 10$.

TABLE B.6 Change in Likelihood to Engage in Excessive Use of Corporal
Punishment: Analysis of High-Risk[a] Participants

Program[b]	t *Tests* Mean Change in Scores		One-Way ANOVA Kruskal-Wallis	
	Mean	*(SD)*	*Mean Rank*	*(Rank Order)*
Alternatives (*n* = 21)	.62	(1.0)**	81.57	(6)
APM (*n* = 16)	1.19	(0.8)***	110.81	(2)
Congreso (*n* = 21)	1.29	(0.6)***	118.74	(1)
Crime Prevention (*n* = 51)	0.55	(0.8)***	73.4	(7)
FSA of Bucks County (*n* = 22)	0.77	(0.8)***	89.2	(4)
FSS (*n* = 21)	.95	(0.8)***	96.64	(3)
YSI (*n* = 26)	.73	(1.1)**	85.23	(5)
			Chi-Square	
All programs (*n* = 178)	.82	(0.9)***	17.6**	

a. Participants rated likely to engage in this behavior.
b. Excludes programs with few high-risk participants: FSP (*n* = 3) and Philadelphia Society (*n* = 5).
**$p < .01$; ***$p < .001$.

TABLE B.7 Change in Likelihood to Engage in Inadequate Supervision: Analysis of High-Risk[a] Participants

Program[b]	t Tests Mean Change in Scores		One-Way ANOVA Kruskal-Wallis	
	Mean	(SD)	Mean Rank	(Rank Order)
Alternatives ($n = 10$)	.50	(0.5)*	70.50	(6)
APM ($n = 16$)	.69	(0.9)**	78.88	(3)
Congreso ($n = 25$)	1.52	(0.7)***	116.28	(1)
Crime Prevention ($n = 34$)	.68	(0.9)***	74.91	(4)
FSA of Bucks County ($n = 16$)	.94	(1.0)**	87.44	(2)
FSS ($n = 17$)	.47	(1.1)	66.06	(7)
YSI ($n = 43$)	.58	(1.1)**	72.05	(5)
			Chi-Square	
All programs ($n = 161$)	.78	(1.0)***	21.23**	

a. Participants rated as likely to engage in this behavior.
b. Excludes programs with few high-risk participants: FSP ($n = 0$) and Philadelphia Society ($n = 1$).
*$p < .05$; **$p < .01$; ***$p < .001$.

TABLE B.8 Change in Likelihood to Be Emotionally Uninvolved: Analysis of High-Risk[a] Participants

Program[b]	t Tests Mean Change in Scores		One-Way ANOVA Kruskal-Wallis	
	Mean	(SD)	Mean Rank	(Rank Order)
Alternatives ($n = 20$)	.75	(0.9)**	80.53	(5)
APM ($n = 10$)	.80	(0.9)*	83.30	(4)
Congreso ($n = 23$)	1.57	(0.7)***	121.85	(1)
Crime Prevention ($n = 55$)	.80	(0.8)***	80.28	(6)
FSA of Bucks County ($n = 18$)	1.17	(0.9)***	101.03	(2)
FSS ($n = 17$)	.94	(1.0)**	88.38	(3)
YSI ($n = 33$)	.70	(1.3)**	78.59	(7)
			Chi-Square	
All programs ($n = 176$)	.93	(1.0)***	15.56*	

a. Participants rated as likely to engage in this behavior.
b. Excludes programs with few high-risk participants: FSP ($n = 3$) and Philadelphia Society ($n = 5$).
*$p < .05$; **$p < .01$; ***$p < .001$.

References

Adoption and Safe Families Act of 1997, Pub. L. 96-272.

Antonucci, T., & Mikus, K. (1988). The power of parenthood: Personality and attitudinal changes during the transition to parenthood. In G. Y. Michaels & A. Goldbery (Eds.), *The transition to parenthood: Current theory and research* (pp. 62-84). New York: Cambridge University Press.

Ayoub, C., Jacewitz, M., Gold, R., & Milner, J. (1983). Assessment of a program's effectiveness in selecting individuals "at risk" for problems with parenting. *Journal of Clinical Psychology, 39,* 334-339.

Barnard, K. (1998, February/March). Developing, implementing, and documenting interventions with parents and young children. *Zero to Three,* 23-29.

Barth, R. (1991). An experimental evaluation of in-home child abuse prevention services. *Child Abuse & Neglect, 15,* 363-375.

Barth, R., Hacking, S., & Ash, J. (1986). Identifying, screening and engaging high-risk clients in private non-profit child abuse prevention programs. *Child Abuse & Neglect, 10,* 99-109.

Barth, R., & Schinke, S. (1984, November). Enhancing the social supports of teenage mothers. *Social Casework: The Journal of Contemporary Social Work,* 523-531.

Baumrind, D. (1992). *Family factors applied to child maltreatment.* Washington, DC: National Research Council.

Beeman, S. (1995). Reconceptualizing social support: The results of a study on the social networks of neglecting mothers. In *Children in the shadows,* proceedings from the Children in the Shadows conference, Minneapolis, MN, March 25, 1994 (pp. 61-84).

Belsky, J. (1980). Child maltreatment: An ecological integration. *American Psychologist, 35,* 320-325.

Belsky, J. (1984). The determinants of parenting: A process model. *Child Development, 55,* 83-96.

Berkeley Planning Associates. (1977). *Child abuse and neglect treatment programs: Final report and summary of findings from the evaluation of the joint OCD/SRS Na-*

tional Demonstration Program in child abuse and neglect, 1974-1977 (prepared for the National Center for Health Services Research under Contracts 106-74-120 & 230-75-0076). Available from Berkeley Planning Associates, 440 Grand Avenue, Oakland, CA 94601.

Berlin, L., O'Neal, C., & Brooks-Gunn, J. (1998, February/March). What makes early intervention programs work? *Zero to Three,* 4-15.

Bradley, R., Whiteside, L., Mundfrom, D., Case, P., Kelleher, K., & Pope, S. (1994). Early indications of resilience and their relation to experiences in the home environments of low birthweight, premature children living in poverty. *Child Development, 65,* 346-360.

Bronfenbrenner, U. (1979). *The ecology of human development.* Cambridge, MA: Harvard University Press.

Brown, S., & English, A. (1998). Health care reform: What America's children need. In *Legislative update: The Adoption and Safe Families Act of 1997.* Chicago: National Committee to Prevent Child Abuse. (Original work printed in 1994)

Browne, K., & Saqi, S. (1988). Approaches to screening for child abuse and neglect. In K. Browne, C. Davies, & P. Stratton (Eds.), *Early prediction and prevention of child abuse* (pp. 57- 85). Chichester, UK: Wiley.

Burgess, R. L. (1979). Child abuse: A social interactional analysis. In B. B. Lahey & A. Kazdin (Eds.), *Advances in clinical psychology, 2* (pp. 142-172). New York: Plenum.

Casanova, G. M., Domaniac, J., McCanne, T. R., & Milner, J. (1992). Physiological responses to non-child-related stressors in mothers at risk for child abuse. *Child Abuse & Neglect, 16*(1), 31-44.

Cicchetti, D., & Lynch, M. (1993). Toward an ecological transactional model of community violence and child maltreatment: Consequences for children's development. *Psychiatry, 56,* 96-116.

Clinton, B. (1992). The Maternal Infant Health Outreach Worker Project: Appalachian communities help their own. In M. Larner, R. Halpern, & O. Harkavy (Eds.), *Fair Start for children: Lessons learned from seven demonstration projects* (pp. 23-45). New Haven, CT: Yale University Press.

Cohn, A. (1983). *An approach to preventing child abuse.* Chicago: National Committee to Prevent Child Abuse.

Cook, T., & Campbell, D. (1979). *Quasi-experimentation: Design and analysis issues for field settings.* Boston: Houghton Mifflin.

Coulton, C., Korbin, J., Su, M., & Chow, J. (1995). Community level factors and child maltreatment rates. *Child Development, 66,* 1262-1276.

Crittenden, P. M. (1985). Social networks, quality of childrearing, and child development. *Child Development, 56,* 1299-1313.

Daro, D. (1988). *Confronting child abuse.* New York: Free Press.

Daro, D. (1991). Building a national child welfare data base: Utilizing a variety of sources. *Protecting Children, 8*(3), 4-6, 24-25.

Daro, D. (1998). *Public opinion and behaviors regarding child abuse prevention: 1998 survey* (Working Paper No. 840). Chicago: Prevent Child Abuse America.

Daro, D., & Gelles, R. (1992). Public attitudes toward abuse. *Journal of Interpersonal Violence, 7*(4), 517-531.

Daro, D., & McCurdy, K. (1994). Preventing child abuse and neglect: Programmatic interventions. *Child Welfare, 5,* 405-430.

Davis, S. M., & Savas, S. A. (1996). Closing the gap: Does the program match the blueprint. In P. J. Pecora, W. R. Seelig, F. A. Zirps, & S. M. Davis (Eds.), *Quality improvements to evaluation in child and family services* (pp. 55-71). Washington, DC: CWLA.

DePanfillis, D. (1996). Social isolation of neglectful families: A review of social support assessment and intervention models. *Child Maltreatment, 1*(2), 37-52.

Downing, D., & Clark, J. (1997). *Statistics the easy way.* Hauppage, NY: Barron's.

Egeland, B., & Jacobvitz, D. (1984). Intergenerational continuity of parental abuse: Cause and consequences. Paper presented at the Conference on Biosocial Perspectives in Abuse and Neglect, York, Maine.

Elder, G., Liker, J., & Cross, C. (1984). Parent and child behavior in the Great Depression. In P. Baltes & O. Brim (Eds.), *Life-span development and behavior* (Vol. 6, pp. 109-158). Orlando, FL: Academic Press.

Epperson, D. L., Bushway, D. J., & Warman, R. E. (1983). Client self-terminations after one counseling session: Effects of problem recognition, counselor gender, and counselor experience. *Journal of Counseling Psychology, 30*(3), 307-315.

Family Preservation and Support Act of 1993, Pub. L. 103-66.

Fink, A., & McCloskey, L. (1990). Moving child abuse and neglect prevention programs forward: Improving program evaluations. *Child Abuse & Neglect, 14,* 187-206.

Fontana, C., Fleischman, A., McCarton, C., Meltzer, A., & Ruff, H. (1988). A neonatal preventive intervention study: Issues of recruitment and retention. *Journal of Primary Prevention, 9*(3), 164-176.

Gabinet, L. (1979). Prevention of child abuse and neglect in an inner-city population: II. The program and the results. *Child Abuse & Neglect, 3*(3/4), 809-818.

Garbarino, J. (1980). Defining emotional maltreatment: The message is the meaning. *Journal of Psychiatric Treatment and Evaluation, 2,* 105-110.

Garbarino, J. (1990). The human ecology of early risk. In S. Meisels & J. Shonkoff (Eds.), *Handbook of early childhood intervention* (pp. 78-96). Cambridge, UK: Cambridge University Press.

Garbarino, J., Dubrow, N., Kostelny, K., & Pardo, C. (1992). *Children in danger.* Coping with the consequences of community violence. San Francisco: Jossey Bass.

Garbarino, J., & Sherman, D. (1980). High-risk neighborhoods and high-risk families: The human ecology of child maltreatment. *Child Development, 51,* 188-198.

Gelles, R. (1989). Child abuse and violence in single-parent families: Parent absence and economic deprivation. *American Journal of Orthopsychiatry, 59*(4), 492-501.

Gelles, R. (1992). Poverty and violence toward children. *American Behavioral Scientist, 35*(3), 258-274.

Gelles, R., & Straus, M. (1988). *Intimate violence.* New York: Simon & Schuster.

Gil, D. (1970). *Violence against children: Physical child abuse in the U.S.* Cambridge, MA: Harvard University Press.

Goldberg, G. (1995). Theory and practice in program development: A study of the planning and implementation of fourteen social programs. *Social Service Review, 69*(4), 614-655.

Gomby, D., Larson, C., Lewit, E., & Behrman, R. (1993). Home visiting: Analysis and recommendations. *The Future of Children, 3*(3), 6-22.

Guterman, N. (1997). Early prevention of physical child abuse and neglect: Existing evidence and future directions. *Child Maltreatment, 2*(1), 12-34.

Hagestad, G., & Neugarten, B. (1985). Age and the life course. In R. Binstock & E. Shanas (Eds.), *Handbook of aging and the social sciences.* New York: Van Nostrand Reinhold.

Halpern, R. (1992). Issues of program design and implementation. In M. Larner, R. Halpern, & O. Harkavy (Eds.), *Fair Start for children: Lessons learned from seven demonstration projects* (pp. 179-197). New Haven, CT: Yale University Press.

Halpern, R. (1993). The societal context of home visiting and related services for families in poverty. *The Future of Children, 3*(3), 158-171.

Halpern, R., & Covey, L. (1983). Community support for adolescent parents and their children: The Parent-To-Parent Program in Vermont. *Journal of Primary Prevention, 3*(3), 160-173.

Hardy, J., & Streett, R. (1989). Family support and parenting education in the home: An effective extension of clinic-based preventive health care services for poor children. *Journal of Pediatrics, 115*(6), 927-931.

Hawaii Department of Health. (1992). *Healthy start.* Honolulu, HI: Author, Maternal & Child Health Branch.

Health Care Coalition on Violence. (1998). *Review of the research on home visitation.* Anoka, MN: Author.

Helfer, R. (1987). The litany of the smoldering neglect of children. In R.E. Helfer & R. Kempe (Eds.), *The battered child* (4th ed., rev.; pp. 301-311). Chicago: University of Chicago Press.

Herzog, E., Cherniss, D., & Menzel, B. (1986). Issues in engaging high-risk adolescent mothers in supportive work. *Infant Mental Health Journal, 7*(1), 59-68.

Hiatt, S., Sampson, D., & Baird, D. (1997). Paraprofessional home visitation: Conceptual and pragmatic considerations. *Journal of Community Psychology, 25*(1), 77-93.

Josten, L. E., Mullet, S. E., Savik, K., Campbell, R., & Vincent, P. (1995). Client characteristics associated with not keeping appointments for public health nursing home visits. *Public Health Nursing, 21*(5), 305-311.

Josten, L., Reckenger, D., Frederickson, B., Savik, K., & Cross, S. (1997). *Client and provider factors associated with keeping initial home visits.* Unpublished manuscript.

Kamerman, S. B., & Kahn, A. J. (1989). *Social services for children, youth and families in the United States.* Baltimore: Annie E. Casey Foundation.

Kaufman, J., & Zigler, E. (1987). Do abused children become abusive parents? *American Journal of Orthopsychiatry, 57*(2), 186-192.

Kitzman, H., Cole, R., Yoos, H. L., & Olds, D. (1997). Challenges experienced by home visitors: A qualitative study of program implementation. *Journal of Community Psychology, 25*(1), 95-109.

Krugman, D. (1993). Universal home visiting: A recommendation from the U.S. Advisory Board on Child Abuse and Neglect. *The Future of Children, 3*(3), 184-191.

Larner, M., Halpern, R., & Harkavy, O. (1992). The Fair Start story: An overview. In M. Larner, R. Halpern, & O. Harkavy (Eds.), *Fair Start for children: Lessons learned from seven demonstration projects.* New Haven, CT: Yale University Press.

Larson, C. (1980). Efficacy of prenatal and postpartum home visits on child health and development. *Pediatrics, 66*(2), 191-197.

Lengua, L., Roosa, M., Schupak-Neuberg, E., Michaels, M., Berg, C., & Weschler, L. (1992). Using focus groups to guide the development of a parenting program for difficult-to-reach, high-risk families. *Family Relations, 41,* 163-168.

Liaw, F., & Brooks-Gunn, J. (1994). Patterns of low birth weight: Children's cognitive development and their determinants. *Developmental Psychology, 23*(4), 360-372.

Liebert, R., & Wicks-Nelson, R. (1981). *Developmental psychology* (3rd ed.). Englewood Cliffs, NJ: Prentice Hall.

Lyons-Ruth, K., Connell, D., Grunebaum, H., & Botein, H. (1990). Infants at social risk: Maternal depression and family support services as mediators of infant development and security of attachment. *Child Development, 61,* 85-98.

Maccoby, E., & Martin, J. A. (1983). Socialization in the context of the family: Parent-child interaction. In P. H. Mussen & E. M. Hetherington (Eds.), *Handbook of child psychology: Socialization. personality. and social development* (pp. 1-102). New York: John Wiley.

MacMillan, H., MacMillan, J., Offord, D., Griffith, L., & MacMillan, A. (1994). Primary prevention of child physical abuse and neglect: A critical review, Part 1. *Journal of Child Psychology and Psychiatry, 35*(5), 835-856.

Marcenko, M., & Spence, M. (1994). Home visitation services for at-risk pregnant and postpartum women: A randomized trial. *American Journal of Orthopsychiatry, 64*(3), 468-478.

McCurdy, K. (1995). Risk assessment in child abuse prevention programs. *Social Work Research, 19*(2), 77-88.

McCurdy, K. (1996). *Home visiting.* Monograph prepared for the National Center on Child Abuse and Neglect, Washington, DC.

McCurdy, K., Hurvis, S., & Clark, J. (1996). Engaging and retaining families in child abuse prevention programs. *APSAC Advisor, 9*(3), 1, 3-8.

McLoyd, V. (1990). The impact of economic hardship on black families and children: Psychological distress, parenting and socioemotional development. *Child Development, 6,* 311- 346.

Milner, J.S. (1986). *The Child Abuse Potential Inventory manual.* Webster, NC: Psytech.

Milner, J. S., Gold, R. G., Ayoub, C., & Jacewitz, M. M. (1984). Predictive validity of the Child Abuse Potential Inventory. *Journal of Consulting and Clinical Psychology, 52,* 879-884.

Milner, J. S., Gold, R. G., & Wimberly, R. C. (1986). Prediction and explanation of child abuse: Cross-validation of the Child Abuse Potential Inventory. *Journal of Consulting and Clinical Psychology, 54,* 865-866.

Mitchel, L. (1990). *The William Penn Foundation Child Abuse Prevention Initiative: Program and community profiles.* Unpublished manuscript. Chicago: National Committee to Prevent Child Abuse.

Myers-Walls, J. A., Elicker, J., & Bandyck, J. (1997, August). *Which families stay and which ones leave an early home visiting program?* Paper presented at the 105th Convention of the American Psychological Association, Chicago, IL.

Nagy, M. C., Leeper, J. D., Hullet-Robertson, S., & Northrup, R. S. (1992). The Rural Alabama Pregnancy and Infant Health Project: A rural clinic reaches out. In M. Larner, R. Halpern, & O. Harkavy (Eds.), *Fair Start for children: Lessons learned from seven demonstrations projects* (pp. 91-114). New Haven, CT: Yale University Press.

Nath, P., Borkowski, J. G., Whitman, T., & Schellenbach, C. (1991). Understanding adolescent parenting: The dimensions and functions of social support. *Family Relations, 40,* 411-420.

National Committee to Prevent Child Abuse. (1990). *William Penn Foundation Prevention Initiative: Comparative case studies.* Chicago: Author.

National Committee to Prevent Child Abuse. (1991). *Study of provider characteristics and attitudes.* Chicago: Author.

National Committee to Prevent Child Abuse. (1992). The William Penn Foundation Prevention Initiative: Final report. Chicago: Author.

National Committee to Prevent Child Abuse. (1996). *Intensive home visitation: A randomized trial follow-up and risk assessment study of Hawaii's Healthy Start Program* (National Center on Child Abuse and Neglect, Grant No. 90-CA-1511). Chicago: Author.

National Research Council. (1993). *Understanding child abuse and neglect.* Washington, DC: National Academy Press.

National Research Council. (1998). *Violence in families: Assessing prevention and treatment programs.* Washington, DC: National Academy Press.

Olds, D., Eckenrode, J., Henderson, C. R., Kitzman, H., Powers, J., Cole, R., Sidora, K., Morris, P., Pettitt, L., & Lucky, D. (1997). Long-term effects of home visitation on maternal life course and child abuse and neglect. *Journal of the American Medical Association, 278,* 637-643.

Olds, D., Henderson, C., Chamberlin, R., & Tatelbaum, R. (1986). Preventing child abuse and neglect: A randomized trial of nurse home visitation. *Pediatrics, 78*(1), 65-78.

Olds, D., Henderson, C., Phelps, C., Kitzman, H., & Hanks, C. (1993). Effects of prenatal and infancy nurse home visitation on government spending. *Medical Care,* 155-174.

Olds, D., & Kitzman, H. (1993). Review of research on home visiting for pregnant women and parents of young children. *The Future of Children, 3*(3), 53-92.

O'Leary, K., Shore, J., & Wieder, S. (1984). Contacting pregnant adolescents: Are we missing cues? *Social Casework: The Journal of Contemporary Social Work, 65,* 297-306.

Owen, G., & Fercello, C. (1998). *Reducing child maltreatment among high-risk families: Executive summary* (Working paper prepared for the McKnight Foundation). St. Paul, MN: Wilder Research Center.

Pecora, P., Haapala, D., & Fraser, M. (1991). Comparing intensive family preservation services with other family-based service programs. In E. Tracy, D. Haapala, J. Kinney, & P. Pecora (Eds.), *Intensive family preservation services: An instructional source book* (pp. 117-142). Cleveland, OH: Case Western Reserve University, Mandel School of Applied Social Sciences.

Perry, B. (1995). Incubated in terror: Neurodevelopmental factors in the "cycle of violence." In J. Osofsky (Ed.), *Children, youth and violence: Searching for solutions* (pp. 87-115). New York: Guilford.

Perry, B., Pollard, R., Blakley, T., Baker, W., & Vigilante, D. (1995). Childhood trauma, the neurobiology of adaptation, and "use-dependent" development of the brain: How "states" become "traits." *Infant Mental Health Journal, 16*(4), 271-291.

Personal Responsibility and Work Reconciliation Act of 1996, Pub. L. 104-193.

Pietrzak, J., Ramler, M., Renner, T., Ford, L., & Gilbert, N. (1990). *Practical program evaluation: Examples from child abuse prevention.* Newbury Park, CA: Sage.

Polansky, N., Gaudin, J., & Kilpatrick, A. (1992). Family radicals. *Children and Youth Services Review, 14,* 19-26.

Powell, D. (1984). Social network and demographic predictors of length of participation in a parent education program. *Journal of Community Psychology, 12,* 13-20.

Powell, D. (1990). Home visiting in the early years: Policy and program design decisions. *Young Children, 45*(6), 65-73.

Powell, D., & Grantham-McGregor, S. (1989). Home visiting of varying frequency and child development. *Pediatrics, 84*(1), 157-164.

Pumariega, A. J. (1996). Culturally competent evaluation of outcomes in systems of care for children's mental health. *TABrief, 2*(2), 1, 3-5.

Ramey, C., Bryant, D., Wasik, B., Sparling, J., Fendt, K., & LaVange, L. (1992). Infant Health and Development Program for low birth weight, premature infants: Program elements, family participation, and child intelligence. *Pediatrics, 3,* 454-465.

Saylor, C., Elksnin, N., Farah, B., & Pope, J. (1990). Depends on who you ask: What maximizes participation of families in early intervention programs. *Journal of Pediatric Psychology, 15*(5), 557-569.

Schorr, L. (1988). *Within our reach.* New York: Anchor/Doubleday.

Schorr, L. (1997). *Common purpose: Strengthening families and neighborhoods to rebuild America.* New York: Doubleday.

Schweinhart, L., Barnes, H., & Weikart, D. (1993). *Significant benefits: The High/Scope Perry Preschool study through age 27* (Monograph 10). Ypsilanti, MI: High/Scope Educational Research Foundation.

Sedlak, A., & Broadhurst, D. (1996). *Third National Incidence Study of Child Abuse and Neglect: Final report.* Washington, DC: U.S. Department of Health and Human Services.

Seitz, V., Rosenbaum, L., & Apfel, N. (1985). Effects of family support intervention: A ten-year follow-up. *Child Development, 56,* 376-391.

Sheldon, T., & Parker, H. (1992). Race and ethnicity in health research. *Journal of Public Health Medicine, 14*(2), 104-110.

Siegel, E., Bauman, K., Schaefer, E., Saunders, M., & Ingram, D. (1980). Hospital and home support during infancy: Impact on maternal attachment, child abuse and neglect, and health care utilization. *Pediatrics, 66,* 183-190.

Slaughter-Defoe, D. (1993). Home visiting with families in poverty: Introducing the concept of culture. *The Future of Children, 3*(3), 172-183.

Spoth, R., Redmond, C., Hockaday, C., & Shin, C. (1996). Barriers to participation in family skills preventive interventions and their evaluations. *Family Relations, 45,* 247-254.

Steele, B. (1976). Violence within the family. In C. H. Kempe & A. E. Helfer (Eds.), *Child abuse and neglect: The family and the community* (pp. 3-24). Cambridge, MA: Ballinger.

Thompson, R. (1995). *Preventing child maltreatment through social support.* Thousand Oaks, CA: Sage.

Tyron, G. S., & Tyron, W. W. (1986). Factors associated with clinical practicum trainees' engagement of clients in counseling. *Professional Psychology: Research and Practice, 17,* 586-589.

U.S. Advisory Board on Child Abuse and Neglect. (1991). *Creating caring communities: Blueprint for an effective federal policy on child abuse and neglect.* Washington, DC: Government Printing Office.

U.S. Advisory Board on Child Abuse and Neglect. (1995). *A nation's shame: Fatal child abuse and neglect in the United States.* Washington, DC: Government Printing Office.

U.S. Department of Health and Human Services. (1998). *Child maltreatment: Reports from the states to the National Child Abuse and Neglect Data Systems.* Washington, DC: Government Printing Office.

U.S. General Accounting Office. (1990). *Home visiting: A promising early intervention strategy for at-risk families* (GAO/HRD-90-83). Washington, DC: Author.

Vondra, J., & Belsky, J. (1993). Developmental origins of parenting: Personality and relationship factors. In T. Luster & L. Okagaki (Eds.), *Parenting: An ecological perspective* (pp. 1-33). Hillsdale, NJ: Lawrence Erlbaum.

Wandersman, L. (1982). An analysis of the effectiveness of parent-infant support groups. *Journal of Primary Prevention, 3*(2), 99-109.

Wang, C. T., & Daro, D. (1998). *Current trends in child abuse reporting and fatalities: The results of the 1997 annual fifty state survey.* Chicago: National Committee to Prevent Child Abuse.

Weiss, C. (1972). *Evaluation research: Methods of assessing program effectiveness.* Englewood Cliffs, NJ: Prentice Hall.

Weiss, C. (1993). Home visits: Necessary but not sufficient. *The Future of Children, 3*(3), 113-128.

Wekerle, C., & Wolfe, D. (1993). Prevention of child physical abuse and neglect: Promising new directions. *Clinical Psychology Review, 13,* 501-540.

Wesch, D., & Lutzker, J. (1991). A comprehensive evaluation of Project 12 Ways: An ecobehavioral program for treating and preventing child abuse and neglect. *Journal of Family Violence, 6*(1), 17-35.

Winters-Smith, C., & Larner, M. (1993). The Fair Start program: Outreach to migrant farm workers. In M. Larner, R. Halpern, & O. Harkavy (Eds.), *Fair Start for children: Lessons learned from seven demonstration projects* (pp. 46-67). New Haven, CT: Yale University Press.

Wolfe, D. (1991). *Preventing physical and emotional abuse of children.* New York: Guilford.

INDEX

About the Authors

Karen McCurdy, PhD, is Assistant Professor in Human Development and Family Studies at the University of Rhode Island. For the past 10 years, she has studied the effects of child abuse prevention programs on parents and children. Currently, she is investigating engagement and retention issues in family support programs and methods to enhance resilience in vulnerable children. She served as a principal analyst for the National Committee to Prevent Child Abuse for 10 years and is Associate Editor for Prevention for the *APSAC Advisor,* a journal of the American Professional Society on the Abuse of Children. She received a PhD in Human Development and Social Policy from Northwestern University.

Elizabeth D. Jones, PhD, is a policy analyst, specializing in welfare reform, within the Executive Office of Planning, Evaluation and Project Management at the Texas Department of Human Services (TDHS). She has over 20 years of experience conducting qualitative and quantitative research and program evaluation in the areas of child abuse prevention, adolescent pregnancy prevention, and improving the educational and employment outcomes for economically disadvantaged mothers. Prior to coming to TDHS, Dr. Jones was Research Director at the Institute for Child and Family Policy at the Edmund S. Muskie School of Public Service, University of Southern Maine. Dr. Jones worked at the National Committee to Prevent Child Abuse during the years 1989 to 1995. She holds a PhD in Sociology from Northwestern University.